Guiding Literacy Learners

Susan Hill

Stenhouse Publishers
York, Maine

I wish to gratefully acknowledge the teachers and children at Gilles Street School in South Australia. Thanks to Chris Hastwell for her warmth and friendship for over thirty years of teaching and learning. – S.H.

ACKNOWLEDGMENTS

Moms and Dads, The merry-go-round, Tiny and the big wave and *The Marble Patch* (PM Collection) reproduced by permission of Nelson Thomas Learning, Australia.

Dogs, Grandpa's House, My Baby Sister, Going Shopping, Animal Diggers and *Insects* (Alphakids) reproduced by permission of Sundance Publishing.

Three Silly Monkeys (Foundations), written by Helen Depree, illustrated by Fraser Williamson, 1995, Melbourne, pp 8–9, copyright © 1995 Helen Depree; *Fast Machines,* (Foundations) written by Peter and Sheryl Sloan, illustrated by Nicola Belsham, 1995, Melbourne, pp 6–7, copyright © 1995 Peter and Sheryl Sloan; *Running,* (Foundations) written by Philippa Jean, illustrated by Brent Putze, 1995, Melbourne, pp 6–7, copyright © 1995 Philippa Jean, reproduced by permission of Macmillan Education Australia.

PM Collection titles (pp. 37, 39, 43 and 46) distributed in the United States of America by Rigby, a division of Reed Elsevier Inc. 500 Conventry Lane Crystal Lake IL 60014, USA.

Alphakids titles (pp. 32, 38, 40 and 45) distributed in the United States of America by Sundance Publishing, 234 Taylor Street Littleton MA 01460, USA.

Foundations titles (pp. 33, 39 and 44) distributed in the United States of America by The Wright Group 19201 120th Avenue NE Bothell WA 98011, USA.

Stenhouse Publishers, P.O. Box 360, York, Maine 03909
www.stenhouse.com

ISBN 1-57110-327-9

First published in 1999
Eleanor Curtain Publishing
906 Malvern Road
Armadale Vic 3143
Australia

Production by Publishing Solutions
Edited by Ruth Siems
Designed by David Constable
Printed in Singapore

Contents

CHAPTER ONE

Introduction to guiding literacy learning

This book is about guiding literacy learning, with a special focus on guided reading. The book explores how teachers can initiate guided literacy that engages and links to children's social worlds. Guiding literacy learning takes place in small groups where teachers work with texts that are chosen to extend children's reading and writing behaviours. To begin, we explore a classroom where a guided reading session is taking place.

In the classroom ...

Five children in a guided reading group sit with their teacher. The group discusses the topic of spiders – a shared interest. The children can read books with simple captions and most have a repertoire of several words they can read by sight. The teacher holds up the book *Spiders* so the children can see the photographs, then encourages talk about spiders while prompting children to use the syntax and vocabulary that appear in the book.

TEACHER: This book is about different kinds of spiders.

CHILD: We had a tarantula in our house once.

CHILD: You shouldn't kill spiders. You get paper to take them outside.

CHILD: We had a spider inside the car on the window.

CHILD: Redback spiders are poisonous.

CHILD: They're not all poisonous, some spiders are friendly.

TEACHER: Do you know the names of some different kinds of spiders?

The conversation continues until most of the ideas about poisonous and safe spiders have been heard, and the new vocabulary and syntax patterns in the book have been used in the children's talk. Then the teacher hands out individual copies of the book and children read the book silently, or softly, individually or in pairs. The book has about 100 words in total and many high-frequency words such as *the*, *as* and *here* that the children can read. As children read the book the teacher listens, observes and plans teaching opportunities based on the children's reading behaviours, perhaps focusing on the word or alphabetic code, the sentence grammar or punctuation, or the different ways to read the particular text type.

A guided reading group

While the teacher works with the guided reading group, the other children in the class are engaged in activities at several literacy learning centres.

In one literacy learning centre, three children read a book aloud in preparation for a readers theatre performance. They have read the book through many, many times and have decided on who will be the narrator, who will read the direct speech, and the number of sentences that each will read before a new reader takes over. They have written a chorus and added various sound effects, and now they are rehearsing because they want to perform the readers theatre for the class in the weekly group sharing time.

A readers theatre group

In another literacy learning centre, several 5- and 6-year-olds are working on a roll movie. They have illustrated a narrative written by the group, and the illustrations have been glued together to make a long strip and placed on a cardboard roll. The group will retell the story orally as they roll the strip through the roll-movie box. The story has been developed from a big book the teacher had read aloud – *Are You My Mother?* – and the children have invented monsters and weird monster names to make the roll movie funny. Over the week this group has negotiated meanings, and reinvented and reworked the problems the character faced, and how they were resolved.

Presenting a roll movie

In another learning centre, children are using one large sheet of paper shaped like a caterpillar to write words with the rime 'ill'. The group members work as individuals, and the words are written with different coloured pens so that the children can check over each other's spelling and give hints about other words to add. There was some discussion about the spelling of the word *gorilla*, and the teacher's advice was sought. At this time the teacher was busy working with a guided reading group, so the children had to solve the problem themselves, which they did by writing the word a few different ways, choosing which version looked right, and then checking the correct spelling in the dictionary.

Group list of 'ill' words

In this classroom, the teacher works with children from twelve different language and cultural groups. All have different cultural and language experiences and these differences are viewed as resources. When language and cultural diversity are viewed as resources, the children act as guides and peer tutors for each other's problem-posing and problem-solving.

The teacher is fascinated by what the children want to talk about and what they notice. She comments that they appear different from children one, two or three decades ago. There is little she can take for granted about their histories or experiences, or the world they are participating in and currently forming. She is witness to the ways children's identities are being constructed before her as they negotiate the intertwining issues to do with language, gender, religion, race and class. The differences among the children often prompt interactions where the children explain their particular views of the world and try to influence others. Negotiating through conflicting and competing ideas is valued as important learning. Experiencing the diverse social worlds of children in the classroom moves the teacher beyond her own familiar comfortable world view.

Each day the teacher uses a similar routine in her literacy program. In the mornings she reads aloud from big books, class-made books or short novels. She also shares reading big books with the whole class and has shared writing based on the big books. There is small-group work in guided reading and guided writing, and also time for independent reading and writing.

Taking part in shared writing

There are eight components to her literacy program:
1 Teacher reads aloud   5 Teacher writes
2 Shared reading   6 Shared writing
3 Guided reading   7 Guided writing
4 Independent reading   8 Independent writing

Components of a literacy program*

Teacher reads

The teacher reads aloud to the class from a range of text types. The purpose is for children to engage with texts pitched at a more complex level than they can read. The texts may be selected to demonstrate how writers develop character, setting and plot in fiction, or ways of organising information in factual texts. Longer texts containing a number of several chapters can be read over several weeks.

Teacher writes

The teacher writes on a white board or chart showing how a writer uses words, sentences and text types to record ideas. The teacher may demonstrate various purposes for writing – for example, to explore and express ideas, to report, to explain, to organise points in an argument, or to list ingredients and record instructions. A range of text types and the purposes of these texts are demonstrated and discussed.

Shared reading

Shared reading is usually a whole-group activity and, although it is led by the teacher, children can participate in the reading in various ways, including choral reading and readers theatre. The focus for shared reading may be to learn how to read various text types, how to solve problems in identifying various words or, at the sentence level, the ways punctuation and grammar are used to communicate meaning. The texts in shared reading may be above the children's independent reading level because there is group support for an individual reader.

Shared writing

Shared writing is usually a whole-group activity where the teacher leads the class in exploring ways of writing various text types, constructing more complex sentences and editing and proofreading spelling and grammar. Often big books using a variety of text types are used as a model for the shared writing session. The children interact with the teacher and each other and contribute to the writing by sharing the pen. Shared writing builds confidence within a group, and can be the starting point for guided writing.

Guided reading

Guided reading involves a teacher working with a small group of four to six children reading individual copies of the same text. The texts are selected by the teacher to be at the children's learning level. The texts have some challenges and the teacher prepares the children to use a range of problem-solving strategies to read them. The texts used over successive sessions should have a careful gradient of difficulty.

Guided writing

Guided writing involves individuals or small groups of students writing a range of text types. The teacher may provide short mini-lessons to demonstrate a particular aspect of text type, grammar, punctuation or spelling. Guided writing is linked to reading and various text types are used as models. Students may use writing frames or templates as a scaffold for writing.

Independent reading

The purpose of independent reading is to build fluency and motivation for reading. Children are encouraged to read texts at their independent reading level so that reading is practiced and fluency is increased. Each child is challenged to read on their own for a sustained period of time.

Independent writing

The purpose of independent writing is to build fluency and motivation, and it is a time to express ideas and experiment. Children can write their own creative pieces. Independent writing provides chances for using different text types and encourages children to investigate and practise a variety of written forms.

---

* The components of a literacy program are gathered from a range of sources (Fountas & Pinnell 1996; Department of Education, Wellington, New Zealand 1985).

The eight components of a literacy program are often integrated in various ways. For example, one week the class visited the local police station. The teacher read aloud books about police work (1), and the books were made available for independent reading (8). She wrote a letter with the whole class (5), asking the police at the local station if the class could visit and the police phoned back to give a time and date. The class also shared the reading of a photographic big book that a previous group made about their visit to the police station (2).

After the visit to the police station, the class as a whole group constructed a recount of the visit on a large whiteboard with the teacher acting as scribe (6). From this, the key vocabulary the children could use in their own writing was discussed and underlined (7). In this way the new vocabulary was introduced in context and each child could then write about different events and things they noticed at the police station visit.

The teacher photocopied the children's individual writing to make a cumulative big book and a set of small books for further shared reading and guided reading. The children read these class-made books in other guided reading sessions.

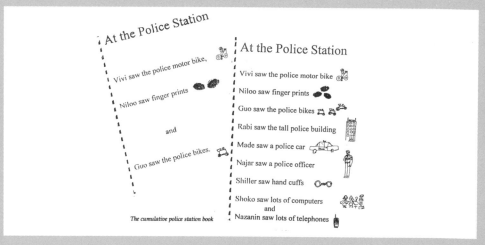

Pages from the cumulative police station book

The classroom is involved with cooperative learning, peer support, partner reading, small-group work, word games, readers theatre – and the expectation that there will be inclusive and equal participation.

In this classroom there are many different school literacies at work, such as formal ways of talking, ways of reading and responding to a story book, ways of talking about non-fiction text, writing a narrative, writing a report and ways of sitting, acting and participating in a group.

The literacy processes of reading and writing inform and complement each other. Reading and writing have much in common because they integrate information from several sources – sounds, letters, syntax and meaning – to communicate meanings.

Reading is ...

Reading begins in the years prior to school and continues into the first years of school and beyond. Beginning readers acquire conceptual knowledge about the uses of print and move to a point where they can read and write independently for purposes that are relevant to them.

Readers are active problem solvers who search for, use, and check against each other, four sources of information while reading for meaning.
- the text meaning – semantics
- the sentence structure – syntax
- the sounds – phonology
- the letters, illustrations, format and layout – visual

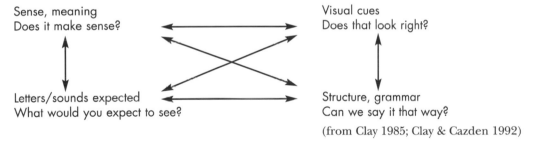

(from Clay 1985; Clay & Cazden 1992)

The endpoint for teaching/reading is to have readers test out a range of problem-solving strategies in order to understand and make sense of the meaning of a text. They use deliberate effort to solve problems with familiar information and procedures. 'They are working with theories of the world and theories about written language, testing them and changing them as they engage in reading and writing activities' (Clay & Cazden 1992: 207).

Readers use a range of literacy behaviours. The differences and difficulty of a text prompt a reader to integrate in different ways the syntactic, visual, semantic and phonological cues. Sometimes the illustrations will be of prime importance; at other times decoding a word will be central. When comprehending a text, the child may challenge how a particular book fits within a known social and cultural world. For example, the fairness of the princess always getting her own way may be debated, and power plays in gender, racial or class stereotypes may be contested.

Taking part in shared reading

In the beginning stages of reading many children learn to work in top gear, integrating cues from several sources and checking them against each other almost simultaneously. Most children learn to shift to a lower gear when texts become difficult and perhaps when they have to attend to a particular set of letter combinations to identify a word. Some children who make slow progress with reading rely on one cue source or a narrow range of strategies. Some rely on the letters and sounds, forgetting about the meaning. Others may rely on the orthography and layout, inventing the text as they go along.

When teachers observe the reading behaviour of their students, they look and listen for the children's use of reading strategies and concepts about print so they can plan for appropriate teaching.

Writing is ...

Writing is similar to reading, and much the same procedure takes place. Writers have to integrate multiple sources of information: the meaning, semantics and syntax; the visual, the graphemes, orthography and layout; the letters and sounds, mapping sounds to letters to create words; structure or grammar of sentences. When children write they work to make speech – what they say – visible.

Children writing – making what they say visible

In addition, writers have an audience in mind – sometimes the teacher and often other children. Children choose their words from those available to them and they face choices with each word that is written: what to write? what not to write? how to get the ideas across? what to say to this person? what to write in school? what is appropriate and what is not?

This is best shown with a diagram based on Dyson (1995) showing the interactive and dynamic nature of writing.

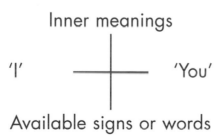

Composing as a dialogic process: its horizontal and vertical dimensions (based on Dyson 1995: 9)

Writing is shaped on one hand by the relationship between the writer and the audience, and on the other hand by the relationship between the speaker's own inner meaning and the signs or words available in the social world. The important notion for early literacy is that different aspects of identity and different relationships with others create different possibilities for speaking and writing.

Children in school learn language as they interact with each other. They take up and use each other's words and the language they may have heard in different contexts. They also use the language from family conversations, stories they have heard, popular songs, their own dramatic play, television and movies. In written language children express their inner meanings, experiences and conflicts by using the signs and words that have been made available to them. This explains why their writing is made up of a range of social dialogue, words, phrases, characters and plots they have heard before. School literacy, which is often more formal than the everyday language used outside of school, has its own vocabulary, syntax and text genres. Children in the early years of school who are developing as writers are also learning to work with more formal conventions.

In the beginning of writing, often the children's oral language races ahead of their mechanical ability to create the words and letters, and so drawing can be used to communicate meanings. Over time, practice with reading and writing provides a broader repertoire of words to use. Both processes are interrelated, and what is learned in one process makes it easier to engage in the other. Reading and writing inform each other.

Guided reading is...

Guided reading is small group instruction with texts selected to scaffold children's literacy development. The teacher introduces and talks through the particular text, then children read while the teacher monitors their reading behaviour. (See later chapters for more details.) After reading, the group returns to the text and the teacher uses pre-planned teaching points or responsive teaching points that may have arisen while the group engaged with the text. As a follow-up there may be a range of literacy learning centres for small groups to further work on the code, text meaning, text genre and format, or critical analysis.

Guided reading is an apprenticeship into the social and cultural practices of literacy (Vygotsky 1978, 1987; Rogoff 1990; Dorn 1998). Children participate in a range of practices and activities with the support of the teacher and peers. When children are apprenticed into literacy in small groups, each child functions at a particular level and has the potential to attain a higher level with the guidance of an adult or a more capable peer(s). The difference between what the child can do alone without help, and what she/he can do with the help of a more expert other is known as the 'zone of proximal development'.

The more proficient partner, the teacher or a peer, may use teaching strategies such as modeling, coaching, scaffolding and encouraging articulation of learning, to guide learning. The teacher, or peer, provides skills and understandings during joint problem solving that are within the child's zone of proximal development and most importantly the problem solving would not be present for the child without the social interaction. In this way the zone of proximal development is dependent on the context and the actual interaction process (Tudge 1992).

In guided reading teachers make connections between children's worlds—their family interests and experiences—and forms of the written text. Guided reading has an important focus on the texts children read, the time engaged in literacy and the tasks that are developed.

Texts

In guided reading the texts are selected to scaffold children's reading development. The texts are supportive and there is some challenge for the children. Many teachers use as a general guide a record of reading behaviour of 90%–95% accuracy when reading a text aloud. The learning level or instructional level of 90–95% accuracy means the text is not too easy, nor too frustrating in difficulty.

The texts in guided reading are selected for a small group of approximately 4–6 children and sometimes the book will appeal to one or two group members more than others. The texts are selected to represent a range of text types and particular teaching points arise from the text. The teaching points may concern decoding, or at times understanding the text structure and text features of, for example, a fable or a report. At other times, critical analysis of the text for accuracy and bias will be a teaching point. In reality, the teaching points on comprehending, decoding and critically analysing the text will overlap.

Time

The amount of time children spend engaged in reading and writing affects achievement in reading and writing. The actual time spent in a guided reading session with the teacher is short—from 5–15 minutes. In a daily literacy block of ninety minutes to two hours, a teacher will meet several guided reading groups. Each guided reading group will meet several times each week so that learning is built upon systematically.

The management of time is important for both teachers and children. The teacher has to schedule to meet several groups of children during each literacy block. The children need to be ready to work with the teacher and more importantly the children have to manage their time and learn to work without the teacher's presence at the various learning centres.

Many teachers suggest that while a particular guided reading session is in progress the rest of the children in the class do not interrupt the group working with the teacher. This means that strategies for ways to solve the problem yourself, such as asking another person, taking a break and coming back to the problem, going on to finish some other work, are explicitly taught to the children.

Tasks

The tasks in guided reading need to be preplanned. The particular text for the group to read is selected and the teaching points can be decided in advance. However, there is flexibility in the planned teaching points as after introducing the book the teacher then observes how the children read the text and ways problems are handled by the children. Based on careful observations, the teacher can then introduce teaching points that demonstrate new, relevant reading strategies, or scaffold and coach children's learning in selected examples of how to read the particular text.

The learning centre tasks can be individual or planned as collaborative activities for pairs or small groups. When children talk through tasks with their peers they are in continuous and constant interaction with others' language and this is one important way that spoken and written language is developed and shaped.

Summary

Guided reading is based on an interactive, dynamic view of literacy in which children learn to read and write through participating in activities which develop their sense of themselves, their language and literacy resources, and cognitive capacities. In this view of learning teachers and children are active constructors of evolving knowledge. It is important to realise that all people do not develop or experience the world in the same way and, importantly for literacy, written texts are worlds held still for a moment, for joint consideration. In fact the literacy learning that the student is engaged in at this very moment is the bridge for the literacy behaviours that can occur in the next second, minute, week and year.

CHAPTER TWO

A procedure for guided reading

Guided reading within a literacy program takes place in small groups where students read texts at a similar level of text difficulty. The teacher supports children's learning through modelling, coaching and scaffolding learning and inviting children to talk about how and what they are learning. Guided reading will look different in different classrooms as teachers modify and change to fit the children and their previous experiences with texts.

Teachers make decisions about the membership of guided reading groups based on their observation of children's reading behaviours. Group membership is flexible and dynamic and some classrooms will have several guided reading groups at a similar level. In multi-age classrooms there may be guided reading groups at the emergent, early, transitional and extending reading phases.

In the classroom ...

This description is of a guided reading group reading a narrative for the first time. Previously the group had read simple caption books with a predictable structure. Chris, the teacher, said about her class: 'The group was at a similar level but with very different strengths. Some children can be pulled up by the others. I chose *The Gingerbread Man* for them to read because I wanted them to read a whole story and they haven't read anything so advanced before. I thought they could read the book because they know the story, as I have read it aloud previously. To get them into the book I first asked them to retell the story.'

She then held up one copy of the small book, sharing the illustrations.

TEACHER	CHILD
Setting the topic, theme and introducing the characters Let's look at the pictures and tell the story about the gingerbread man.	
Who's making gingerbread?	The mum.
Who lives with the mum?	The dad is looking at the gingerbread man.
Providing syntax model When we read we say	
'The little old	The little old man ... and the little old woman *(The teacher joins in with this too)*
... the little old woman.	
Prompting active constructive activity Then what happens?	The little old woman makes the gingerbread man.
What ... how do they cook him?	They cook him in the oven.
Now what does he do when they open the door?	He run away.
Providing syntax model He runs away.	He runs away.
Prompting active constructive activity And what does he say? Do you remember the story?	Run as fast as I can.
Providing syntax model Run, run as fast as you can.	Run, run as fast as you can. You can't catch me I'm the gingerbread man. *(Teacher and children join in together)*

The whole book is then talked through and children discuss the characters the gingerbread man meets; the introduction of the cow, the pig and the fox follows the repetitive predictable pattern of syntax. Chris draws the children's attention to the speech bubbles in the illustrations and they read some of these together.

The children receive a copy of the book and begin to read.

CHILDREN (HALIL AND VIVI)

One day the little old man said, 'I'm h ...

TEACHER

(Rubs her stomach as a prompt.) [*Later the teacher said she should have focused on the text, not drawn attention away from the words on the page.*]

I'm hungry ...
The little old woman said, 'I will make you a gingerbread man.'
And so she did.
The gingerbread man ran away.
'Stop gingerbread man. We want to eat you,' said the little old man and the little old woman.

The gingerbread man did not stop. He ran and he ran and he ran.

Can you point to where the word said 'he' and read it again.

He ran and ran and ran.
He said, 'Run, run a...
ask ...
Run, run a...

Have a look at the letters. Read it again from the top. /a/ ... /s/ ...

as ...

Run, run as fast as you can. You can't catch me I am the gingerbread man.

Let's have a look at this word. *(Points to I'm.)*

You can't catch me I'm the
gingerbread man.

The gingerbread man came to a
... cow. *(Checked illustrations)*

He run and he run ...   Why am I pointing to this word?

... ran ...

He ran and he ran.
He eat the gingerbread man up.   Today I eat yesterday I ...

ate ...

He ate the gingerbread man up.

As the group reads Chris prompts and encourages individual children. They all chose to read differently. Ayme was a little removed
from the group and read silently, mouthing the words but keeping
pace with the more verbal readers. Andrea turned her back on the
group and read to herself, appearing not to want to be distracted by
the other children. Halil read out aloud, salivating with the tension
of getting the reading right and almost shouting, but he was so
engaged it was impossible to ask him to be more quiet. Vivi echoed
Halil and when Halil stumbled on a word Vivi helped him out. In the
transcript of the session it was clear that Chris focused on observing
Halil and Vivi. When Chris pointed to a word she used either of the
two books and both children looked at the same text.

When the book was finished Ayme asked to read it again. She said
'I love this book. Can I take it home?' All the children wanted to take
the book home to read to their families – and they did.

Chris's <u>teaching focus,</u> selected before the guided reading session, was
the characters and plot sequence in the narrative story. After the book
had been read, she asked the children to list all the characters in the
sequence in which they were introduced, and she wrote their names in
order of appearance.

The following work in the literacy learning centre was to make a concertina book which Chris had prepared by folding beforehand.

Concertina book

The children drew pictures of the characters: the gingerbread man, the old woman, the old man, the cow, the pig and the fox. They drew speech balloons and invented sentences and phrases like 'I'd love to eat you', 'I like eating …', 'Yum yum.'

The teaching focus in guided reading is always selected within the context of reading a whole text. For example, if the focus is teaching how to identify a particular word then it is necessary to check to see what word would make sense in that particular sentence. Words are always introduced in context and not taught out of context before the text is read. Getting stuck on teaching words out of context is a serious threat to accelerating reading as what is required in effective reading is the integration – not separation – of multiple information sources.

Teachers ask many questions of themselves before selecting books and working in guided reading sessions:

- What does this group need to learn now?
- What will this group learn from this text?
- What kind of reader is this book written for?
- What does the author want the readers to think?
- What is the world view of the author and illustrator?
- What do I need to do to make connections between the text and children's worlds?
- What other texts can I use to make these links?
- Can I link this text to another that is the same or different?
- What follow-up activities can be provided?
- What teaching focus should I take?
- How can I encourage more conversation and greater negotiation of meaning?
- What in this book might the children know more about than the teacher?

- When should I back off and let the children talk and challenge each other?
- What small-group work or paired work can be devised?

The following procedure outlines what can occur in a guided reading session. It is a guide only, and should be modified to respond to different groups.

A procedure for guided reading

1 Selecting an appropriate text

Texts are selected by relating them to the children's worlds, and their interests and reading behaviours. Many teachers find it is important to read the text through before the session, noting any text features, words or sentence structure that could challenge readers or be unfamiliar to them. These features may provide a teaching focus. Books can be deliberately selected to challenge the group in some way.

2 Getting ready for reading

The topic of the book or the title is discussed. The teacher connects the book to the children's prior social and cultural experiences, makes connections to other books read, and may provide a simple experience to enable children to develop ideas related to those in the book. For example, if the book is about video games then children can briefly share their experiences of such games.

Too much talk at this stage can be confusing and take away from the topic of the text so it is necessary to select a focus and only talk about what is necessary for the children to undertake the reading successfully.

3 Talking through the book

Talking through the book may sound like casual conversation but this is where the teacher talks through the plot of a fiction text, or the organisation of a factual book, providing enough support to enable readers to use the reading strategies they know to draw on information sources in the book.

Talking through the book does not mean the teacher takes over and does all the work such as:

Now I'm going to tell you the story of ....

Nor is this the place for the teacher to answer questions like the following:

And what happened next ...?

And then what ...?

And then ...?

Talking through the book is where questions are posed so that the children can talk about what *they* know, not what the teacher knows. The teacher uses any new words and repeats sentence patterns from the book to provide support, or scaffolding, and this enables the readers to use their own world knowledge while drawing on the cues in the book. Talking through the book alerts the group to the importance of different text types that may require different ways of reading.

Talking through the book: children talking about what they know

To introduce the book, teachers may:

- ask children to summarise the storyline (after looking at the illustrations)
- ask children to talk through each page telling the story from the illustrations
- ask questions that cue the readers to the sentence structure

For example, in preparation for a book that uses a question-and-answer format, the teacher may ask questions to draw attention to the book's question-and-answer sentence structure:

TEACHER: Who is the tallest child in this class?
CHILD 1:   Jake is the tallest.
CHILD 2:   Zac is the tallest.
TEACHER: Zac is the tallest.

The teacher and the small group work in this way to rehearse the book so that when it is read the children have a range of strategies to draw on. Sometimes it helps to repeat the words a child may say if the words are a model of the syntax to be read. This is also the place to clarify any confusion or ambiguity about the book.

4 Reading the book

Children read the book silently or softly, and usually individually while the teacher observes each child's reading behaviours. The teacher may select an additional teaching focus based on these observations.

Prompts can be used to encourage children to integrate visual, phonological, syntactic and semantic cues. These prompts are designed to help the reader solve problems and include:

What do you expect to read?
Does that make sense?
Well done. You made it. That makes sense.
What would sound right here?
Make your mouth ready to say the words.
Check the illustration.
What is the same about this word and [another known word]?
Which page will you read first?
Which way will you go?
As you read, match the words with what you say.
Check the beginning of the word.
It could be ____ but look at the first letter.

The teacher can move from child to child, asking the child to read small sections of the text aloud. This allows some assessment of progress to be made.

The teacher may note a child who is having particular difficulty with the text and set aside time later to take a record of reading behaviours with that child.

The teacher often prompts the children into active constructive reading of the text, linking the book to other experiences by asking questions such as 'Have you ever done that? Have you ever felt like that?' Sometimes the teacher uses a pause to encourage the child to search for information without telling the word quickly. Sometimes an analogy is used, for example to guess the word *other* by saying it's like the word *mother*. Questions and prompts such as this are not just to arouse the child's interest or motivation. These prompts are signals to the child that reading requires active interaction with texts and bring relevant experiences and knowledge to the child's 'context in the mind' (Clay & Cazden 1992).

5 Teaching opportunities

The selected teaching focus provides additional support after the children have read the book. It is useful to select only one or two main teaching points for each guided reading session. Teachers should ensure that, in time, the teaching opportunities selected allow children to develop the reading practices of meaning maker, code breaker, text user and text critic (see page 48).

Teaching opportunities arise in context

The teaching focus will be planned but it will also be adjusted to respond to the children's reading behaviours and the text being read. For example, it might be important to plan the discussion of new written language conventions such as the use of an exclamation mark. However, also be alert to children's unexpected responses as these show learning in action. Some groups might need to focus attention on similarities and differences in high-frequency words such as *with* and *which*. In some texts phonemic awareness is a teaching focus, for example discussing the /sh/ in *fish*. In other texts, making analogies between the known word *fish*, and unknown words *dish, wish* and *swish* may be opportune.

Adjusting teaching opportunities to fit the child

6 Further understanding of the text

After reading the text, the teacher can pose questions that extend the children's comprehension. For example, as meaning maker, the teacher might ask questions exploring the literal, inferential and critical understanding of the text.

Some books will demand analysis of the content with children acting as a text critic. Children may talk about how the text positioned them as someone who knows about the topic or someone who knows little about the topic. Questions could be posed about what or who have been included in the book and the choices the author made when writing the book.

7 Literacy learning centres

Literacy learning centres allow children to practise, consolidate and extend the reading behaviours they have been introduced to in the guided reading sessions. Providing activities which are closely related to the book allows children to engage with the same book for a number of sessions. Many learning centre activities are guided writing sessions.

Children involved in a learning centre activity

Mum is a teacher.

| Mum | is | a | teacher. |

Mum is a teacher.

Dad is a builder.

| Dad | is | a | builder. |

Dad is a builder.

Mum is a policewoman.

| Mum | is | a | policewoman. |

Mum is a policewoman.

Creating texts in a learning centre

CHAPTER THREE

Modelling, scaffolding, coaching and talking

When children learn to read and write they actively build theories about the world and about written language, and they test hypotheses as they go. Therefore, the interactions children have around texts need to be based on active problem-solving, not passive learning. Children who are passive and don't work at problem-solving in reading and writing may fail to make progress. Changing passive learners into dynamic active learners demands careful teaching strategies where the learner learns to do the work and not have someone do it for them.

Modelling, scaffolding, coaching and talking about learning are all teaching strategies that promote active attention to print, and they can all take place in one teaching session.

In the classroom ...

In this example, Barb, a teacher of 5- and 6-year-old children, makes connections between the children's worlds and literacy learning, and uses modelling, scaffolding, coaching and talking about learning when making a large class book. The school where Barb works has a high percentage of transient children and they are not always an easy group to work with. Using the knowledge children bring to school is her starting point.

In the classroom the Nintendo video game and cartoon character Mario were hugely popular. In free writing the children wrote lots of stories based on Mario, a monkey character who jumps over walls, climbs trees and avoids all kinds of fantastic mishaps. The peer culture fascination with Nintendo influenced the whole class who were involved in retelling the game, and the children would go on writing for pages and pages.

Barb found a book called *Power and Glory* that used the same video action sequences as the Mario game. She read it to the class. This provided a model for how a book about a video game might look. Barb pointed out the features of the clever layout of the book where the background changed but the characters stayed the same, as in many video games. This book was requested over and over again because the children loved it.

Next the class, with Barb, decided to make a class game-book based on the video game character. Using skilful teaching, she suggested that everybody in the classroom have an input on how the game-book would work and what the character would be. Everyone in the class talked about what kinds of characters appear in video games and they drew their own imagined characters, displayed them and then voted on one for the class to use. The character was photocopied onto a page for each child ready to simulate a video game. Everyone in the class contributed to drawing background pictures for the pages.

Barb asked questions such as 'What words will be in the book?', 'Will the same words be used over and over again?' and 'If the same words were used again and again, would this be boring?' The children decided they needed lots of verbs because the plot was so action packed. To generate the words they placed all the pictures along the walls of the classroom and listed other words for *run, like, climb, jump.* Every day they would say, 'I've some new words that we could use.'

The class game-book was called *The Adventures of the Poison Toad*. It uses the language rhythm of the video game, and the vocabulary to describe actions – 'sit on the rocks', 'jump the pipe', 'grab the key', 'sweep the rocks', and when there is danger or an exciting part, phrases are repeated several times: 'the witch appeared', 'the witch appeared', 'the witch appeared', 'Zap the witch'. The book was wildly successful, because the children were involved in its construction and they loved the rhythmic read-aloud pattern of the text and also because they loved the Nintendo game.

In this example the teacher drew on popular culture as a way of making connections to school literacies, and the literacy learning worked across several text types in an interactive way. When the teacher and the children made the game-book, they started with the video game, then read a book, then made a book.

In the example, it appears that the events just flowed without much active support from the teacher, but the opposite was true. The teacher actually held back a little and used an approach where the teacher and learner work together to create a meaningful interaction around an event. She modelled how the text worked and provided clear examples of the text features. She used careful intervention to scaffold learning, for example 'Read it again and see if it makes sense ... Does it make sense now?' 'Look at the first letter.' She coached the children, saying 'I like the new words you are writing', 'I like the way you fixed that error', ' How could you fix that problem? Good, that works well.'

The learners participated by setting the goals for the task and they were encouraged to make lots of decisions along the way. The teacher analysed the children's level of independent functioning on tasks, discovered their intentions for solving the task, and coached as support. At times she used questions to clarify purposes or goals for the activity and, when the task was underway, she decided whether it was necessary to model or demonstrate important processes or principles that would enable the task to take place successfully. The activities involved problem-solving, but the key principles for success were clearly demonstrated to the children.

Many teachers guard against doing all the work for children and this is particularly important in the beginnings of literacy. In an article by Askew and Fountas (1998: 133), the authors state that '[w]e must be careful not to establish a pattern early on where the child waits for us to do the work.' Children from the beginning need to learn that they must work at points of difficulty in a text and some initiative is necessary. It is finding the balance between providing enough support and not doing too much that is what skilful teaching is all about.

The modelling, scaffolding, coaching and talking about learning that a teacher engages in encourage children to:

- monitor their own reading and writing
- discover text features and aspects about words for themselves
- search for and use multiple sources of information
- check one source of information against another
- detect and self-correct errors if necessary
- use a range of strategies to read and write new words in texts

Children require a repertoire of strategies to use when they read and write, and these develop over time. To solve problems with text they learn to choose from this repertoire to suit particular problems. Askew and Fountas (1998) cite Clay's (1991) observations of reading behaviours which show the complex set of strategies readers display to solve new words in reading:

- making an estimate that is right
- making estimates that are wrong, noticing them and correcting them
- selecting rapid or slow processing to facilitate the use of information
- attending more fully to selected features of the text as needed
- choosing to search for just enough information to solve the problem
- deriving unknown words by analogy from known words
- partially sounding words and completing these using meaning cues
- sounding parts and linking to other known words
- asking for help

Children can be shown how to use a repertoire of strategies and responsive teaching – teaching that responds to what the learners' intentions are – is essential in dynamic active learning.

Modelling

The teacher, Chris, observed the children as they came to unfamiliar words and decided that it was important to model how to use a learning strategy based on analogy to read an unfamiliar word. To teach the use of analogy, she reads from a small guided reading book. She stops at a word and pretends she doesn't know what it is.

TEACHER: When I came to the word 'strife' I didn't know it. I thought of other words that have the same beginning or ending. What other words have the same end pattern?

CHILDREN: Wife, life, knife ...

Chris writes these words on a chart.

TEACHER: Some other words I know start the same way as the new word – 'strange', 'strong'. So if I put the beginning 'str' together with the ending 'ife' I have a new word 'strife'. So I use what I know from other words to work out the new word.

Chris uses 'whole-to-parts phonics' – the use of analogy or known words to get to new or unfamiliar words. Moustafa (1997) writes about whole-to-parts phonics in the book *Beyond Traditional Phonics*. If, for example, a child can read *fly* and *crub*, then by comparing and contrasting word parts the word *cry* can be read. If a child can read *do* and *unhappy*, then the word *undo* can be read. Explicit language is used to describe and model these processes, and this provides a way of performing complex skills and a guide for supporting independent practice.

The learning strategies for identifying new words are always demonstrated in the context of a whole text that the children have shared with the teacher. In this way, one information source can be isolated and explored briefly, but not dwelt on, as the most important teaching idea is to integrate multiple information sources, not just one.

Modelling the reading process

Coaching

Coaching occurs when the teacher observes literacy events in progress and offers hints, reminders, prompts and gentle pushes to support the learner to solve problems. Sometimes coaching occurs when the teacher observes effective problem-solving such as monitoring reading and self-correcting, and she draws attention to the use of these appropriate strategies. Prompts are particularly useful in helping a child to integrate several sources of information and to apply strategies for working out solutions.

If, for example, a child read the word *duck* for *canary*, the teacher might say:

Duck is a useful word here but look at the first letter 'c'.
Can you think of a word that would fit?
Try the word.
That was a good attempt.
Did it work?
Does it make sense to start with the first letter?

Coaching occurs when the teacher accepts a child's partially correct response and suggests a strategy. For example:

CHILD (*reads*): The three little pigs cried 'Not by ... my chinny chin chin.'

TEACHER: I liked the way you read that, but did you notice that there were some other words there?

At other times, coaching occurs by noticing and commenting on the correct use of particular features such as:

TEACHER: It was a good idea to use the first letter to get to that word.

Coaching is encouraging the continuation of particular problem-solving strategies and dealing positively with any slips or errors. The control and management of the reading process is left more and more to the reader who is coached to become independent and fluent.

Scaffolding

In scaffolding, a temporary structure is provided that enables a child to accomplish an action successfully. The scaffold provides the minimum amount of support. For example, a child has read the word *home* for *place* and the teacher decides that the child needs more careful attention to the visual pattern of the two words. The teacher might say:

Take a good look at the word.
What does it begin with?
What is the last part of the word?
Can you make the word with plastic letters?

Explicit language is used to direct the child to the source of information required in order to solve the problem at hand. The teacher adjusts the support to accommodate the child's increased control. Scaffolding also takes place with texts that are designed so that children learn to problem-solve with support.

In reading, scaffolding support means selecting texts with a gradient of difficulty then teaching by scaffolding questions and comments to support successful reading. For example, these texts are levelled for conceptual difficulty, syntax and vocabulary, complexity, and the amount of support from the illustration and would be used in guided reading within small groups.

A level 1 text: *Dogs* (Alphakids), Sundance 1999, pp.4–5

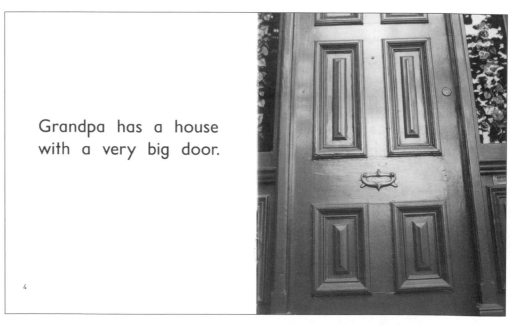

A level 2 text: *Grandpa's House* (Alphakids), Sundance 1998, pp. 4–5

**I can run
faster than
Con and Max and Lee.**

A level 3 text: *Running* (Foundations), The Wright Group 1995, pp. 6–7

Talking about learning

Talking about learning can focus on discussing ways of problem-solving in reading and writing processes, such as how words were identified or what strategies were used to spell a word. Talk can also focus on reflecting about how children work together in literacy learning centres. Talking about learning brings learning strategies to a conscious level where they can be drawn on again and again.

When children talk about how they solved problems when reading a new word they become more aware of their own cognitive processes. For example, as emergent readers learn to attend to particular words they could be asked questions such as:

How did you know what that word was?

What did you use to work out the word?

How did you know that word was different from this one?

There is an issue of balance here. Too much talk about how problems have been solved can take away valuable time from engagement in reading and writing. As well, if the child already knows how to use a particular strategy then talking about it may not be useful.

Asking questions like the following prompts self-reflection:

How could you improve next time?

Show me the part you like best?

Where is your best page?

Which part was the hardest part?

How did you work in your group?

Talking about learning helps children to become conscious of the range of available learning strategies. It is also a way for children to articulate and understand the progress they are making.

Talking about learning: helping children to become conscious of a range of learning strategies

CHAPTER FOUR

Scaffolding with text levels

One of the most important ideas in guided reading is the selection of texts with an ever-increasing gradient of difficulty, and the same idea is important in guided writing. Texts should be selected at the edge of both children's competencies in the small groups and the individual child's continually changing zone of development.

Texts that have a gradient of complexity work to create steady reading and writing progress by drawing the reader's attention to increasingly complex print features.

In the *emergent* reading phase, children read for meaning while attending to directionality, word-to-word matching, reading known words and locating new words. They begin to pay close attention to print, noticing many features of words and letters.

The *early* reading phase builds on and extends the emergent phases by slowly increasing the complexity of concepts in the various text types, sentence structures and words introduced. In the early phases, the length of the sentences and the text increases and the placement of text on the page varies.

In the *transitional* and *extending* phases of reading, the texts should first of all be good stories that build mileage and provide practice. The reader has to orchestrate the use of multiple cues and is consolidating a large repertoire of problem-solving strategies.

The text difficulty levels are based on:
- complexity of concepts in the texts
- complexity of syntax and vocabulary
- length of text
- amount of text on a page
- size and placement of text on a page
- the amount of contextual support in the illustrations

Many teachers organise books into levels of difficulty so that children get sufficient practice from several texts at their instructional or learning level. Teachers can use the following features both to select appropriate texts and as a possible teaching focus for guided reading.

Emergent reading behaviours

The following emergent reading behaviours are just some that teachers may observe:

Concepts about print	Strategic thinking
• knows where to start • understands that print records a message • moves through the text from front to back • moves left-to-right across the page with a return sweep • can point to the title • can point to the author's name • can identify the top and bottom of a page • understands the concept of first, next and last • understands the concept of a word • can identify first, last, next letter • understands the concept of capital and lower case letters • can identify sounds in spoken language • can identify first, last, next sound in spoken language • is aware of punctuation: comma, question mark, exclamation mark, quotation mark, full stop • understands the concept of a sentence • can match story and picture • notices and interprets detail in pictures • matches word-by-word, indicated by precise pointing • matches initial sound and letter • makes one-to-one sound and letter match in written language • can identify letters of the alphabet • can identify some high-frequency words	• predicts what makes sense • makes links between prior knowledge and texts • integrates several cueing sources • searches illustrations, print, structure or memory for meaning • understands some text forms and genres • uses 'book language' • pays close attention to print, noticing some features of letters and words • can map several sounds to letters or letter clusters in writing • can map letters or letter clusters to sounds in reading • makes one-to-one matching of spoken and written word • self-corrects when reading • notices similarities and differences in words and letters • locates familiar and new words • persists in problem-solving • selects appropriate books • remembers familiar sentence structures • uses knowledge of syntax as a source of information • self-monitors by using word-by-word matching • notices known words in a text, or notices mismatches in meaning or language • explores the author's message in a text

Emergent text features

By organising texts in levels with a careful gradient that slowly increases in complexity, children get sufficient practice from several texts at their own instructional level. The texts work to create steady reading progress by drawing the reader's attention to increasingly complex print features. (Text levels are based on Petersen 1991 and Fountas & Pinnell 1996.)

LEVEL 1

- direct match between text and illustration
- high-frequency words are used throughout the text
- book language is used but also some 'oral' vocabulary and syntax
- simple story line
- most books have one line of text per page
- consistent format
- easy-to-follow layout
- ample space between words so children can point and read
- print is regular and easy to see, and clearly separated from the pictures
- text is always printed on a light background
- illustrations promote further discussion
- range of punctuation: capital letters, full stops, exclamation marks, question marks

Mom is a bus driver.

An example of a level 1 emergent text: *Moms and Dads* (Rigby PM Collection), Rigby 1996, pp. 2–3

LEVEL 2

Many features from level 1 plus additional features such as:
- sentence length begins to vary

- texts often have two lines of print on a page – one sentence with a return sweep
- text is predictable and repetitive
- a new sentence structure or twist may be introduced on the last page
- illustrations support and extend the text
- book handling behaviours such as left-to-right directionality, one-to-one word matching, searching for meaning in the pictures

My baby sister can read.
She can read with me.

An example of a level 2 emergent text: *My Baby Sister* (Alphakids), Sundance 1999, pp. 4–5

LEVEL 3

Many characteristics from level 1 and 2 plus additional features such as:
- introduction of longer texts
- increasing variation in sentence structure, book format and layout
- increase in the number of repeated words in a book to provide reading practice
- repetition, refrains and predictable patterns of text
- opportunities to attend to initial letters and word endings
- the core of high-frequency words is increased
- introduction of direct speech
- illustrations still provide support for text although picture format begins to vary
- illustrations may be one or two on a page

Dad said,
"Here is a car, Nick."

"No!" said Nick.

An example of a level 3 emergent text: *The merry-go-round* (Rigby PM Collection), Rigby 1996, pp. 8–9

LEVEL 4

Many characteristics from level 1–3, plus additional features such as:

- text extent increases – one to five lines of text may appear on a page
- print may appear on both left and right pages but is still clearly separated from the illustrations
- phrasing is supported by print placement and line breaks
- frequently encountered words are used more often
- texts use patterns and repetition; others support prediction through use of oral-language-like structures, which may be repeated
- increasing variation in language patterns, requiring children to attend closely to print at several points
- longer sentences use simple and easy-to-understand syntax
- more of the story is carried in the text, but illustrations still support and add to the text

A bus is a machine.
It goes on land.
It can carry people,
and it can go fast.

An example of a level 4 emergent text: *Fast Machines* (Foundations), The Wright Group 1995, pp. 6–7

LEVEL 5

- concepts continue to be within the children's experience and any challenging new ideas have both pictorial and text support (through repetition)
- between one and five lines of text on a page
- increasing variety in sentence length and structure
- new words introduced are often repeated, and words used in earlier texts recur
- use of complex high-frequency words: *under, over, on*
- frequent use of direct speech including the pattern of 'asked and said' in question-and-answer dialogue
- contractions are used often
- use of inflections: 'ing' and 'ed'
- punctuation includes quotation marks
- maps or diagrams may be introduced
- text extent may be less because the structural load is higher

An example of a level 5 emergent text: *Going Shopping* (Alphakids), Sundance 1999, pp. 12–13

Early reading behaviours

Early reading behaviours include developing concepts of how print works, and thinking strategically about making meaning from texts. Concepts of how print works include understanding what a word is, what a letter is, directionality of print and the terms *first, last, top* and *bottom* which are used to explain print layout and placement. Strategic thinking involves integrating several cue sources, searching for meaning and self-correcting, and changing the type of reading to fit different text types such as fiction and factual texts.

The following early reading behaviours are some that teachers may observe:

Concepts of how print works	Strategic thinking
• knows where to start • knows that print records a message • moves through the text from front to back • moves left-to-right across the page making a return sweep • can point to the title • can point to the author's name • can identify top and bottom of a page • understands the concept of word • knows the concept of first, next and last word or letter • understands the concept of capital and lower case letters • identifies sounds in spoken language • can identify first, last, next sound in spoken language • is aware of punctuation: comma, question mark, exclamation mark, quotation mark, full stop • can match story and illustration • notices and interprets detail in illustration • can match word-by-word, indicated by precise pointing • matches initial sound and letter, and makes one-to-one sound and letter match • makes one-to-one sound and letter matching in written language • can identify letters of the alphabet • can identify many high-frequency words	• predicts what makes sense • make links between prior knowledge and texts read • integrates several cueing sources • searches illustrations, print, structure or memory for meaning • understands several text types • uses 'book language' • pays close attention to print, noticing some features of letters and words • can map sounds to letters or letter clusters in writing and reading • makes one-to-one matching of spoken and written word • self-corrects when reading • can make analogies between known words and unfamiliar words • notices similarities and differences in words and letters • locates familiar and new words • persists in problem-solving • selects appropriate books • remembers familiar sentence structures • uses knowledge of syntax as a source of information • self-monitors by using word-by-word matching • notices known words in a text, or notices mismatches in meaning or language • explores and critiques the author's message in a text

Early text features

LEVELS 6–8

Complexity of concepts in the texts:
- the concepts are usually familiar
- topics begin to extend children's knowledge
- increase in the range of text types to include different fiction and factual genres

Complexity of syntax and vocabulary:
- increased variety in vocabulary and syntax
- amount of book language increases
- punctuation includes commas, full stops, exclamation marks, question marks and direct speech
- high-frequency words are extended and used often
- direct speech continues to provide oral language patterns

Length of text:
- amount of text on a page increases
- amount of text on a page varies from one line to ten or eleven lines
- text extent is longer when there is repetition
- text is shorter when the conceptual load is more complex

Size and placement of text on a page:
- print size remains constant
- different placement of text on a page
- clear spacing between words and sentences
- line breaks are designed to support fluent reading
- print appears on both the left- and right-hand pages
- different fonts and font sizes are used within the illustrations

Contextual support in the illustrations:
- most of the story is carried in the illustrations
- illustrations correspond to the text
- increasing variety in the types of illustration
- combinations of illustration may be used, for example photography and drawing
- diagrams are used to label and organise information

Notice
Dogs must be
on a leash.

Mom and Dad and Matt
went for a walk with Tiny.

Tiny ran all the way
down to the beach.

An example of a level 6–8 early text: *Tiny and the big wave* (Rigby PM Collection), Rigby 1997, pp. 2–3

LEVELS 9–11

Many of the text features from levels 6–8 are repeated and the texts become a little longer and more complex.

Complexity of concepts:

- topics are slightly more complex, but still easy to understand
- an increase in the range of text fiction genres, for example folk tales, realistic fiction, raps and rhymes and cumulative stories
- an increase in the range of factual texts, for example information reports, instructions and explanations

Complexity of syntax and vocabulary:

- sentences may contain one or two ideas
- more variety in vocabulary and syntax
- the amount of figurative language increases
- a full range of punctuation is included
- high-frequency words are extended
- direct speech continues to provide oral language patterns
- an increase in the use of inflectional endings *-ed, -ing, -s.*

Length of text:

- sentences are generally a little longer
- variety in sentence length with some short and some long sentences
- amount of text on a page increases
- text extent is longer when there is sentence and phrase repetition
- text is shorter when the conceptual load is more complex

Size and placement of text on a page:

- print size remains constant
- more variety in text placement with some pages with one line of text and some with several lines of text

- clear spacing between words and sentences
- line breaks are designed to support fluent reading
- print appears on both the left- and right-hand pages
- different fonts and font sizes are used within the illustrations

Contextual support in the illustrations:

- illustrations remain supportive but more attention to the print is required
- increasing variety in the types of illustration
- may be several illustrations on each page
- combinations of photography and drawing may be used
- diagrams and maps continue to be used to label and organise information

An example of a level 9–11 early text: *Three Silly Monkeys* (Foundations), The Wright Group 1995, pp. 8–9

Transitional reading behaviours and text features

In transitional reading, children are moving towards becoming more fluent and they have a wider repertoire of problem-solving strategies. The use of multiple cues to get meaning becomes closely orchestrated.

Many of the features from levels 9–11 texts occur in transitional texts and the texts become a little longer and more complex. The more children read, the more practice they get with orchestrating the use of multiple cues to find meaning.

Complexity of concepts:

- topics become more complex
- range of fiction and factual texts

Complexity of syntax and vocabulary:

- sentences may contain one or two ideas
- more variety in vocabulary and syntax
- amount of figurative language increases

- a full range of punctuation is included
- an increase in the use of inflectional endings *-ed, -ing, -s.*

Length of text:
- sentences are generally a little longer
- variety in sentence length with some short and some long sentences
- amount of text on a page increases
- text is longer when there is sentence and phrase repetition
- text is shorter when the conceptual load is more complex

Size and placement of text on a page:
- print size can vary
- more variety in text placement with some pages with one line of text and some with several lines of text
- different fonts and font sizes are used within the illustrations

Contextual support in the illustrations:
- greater attention to the print is required
- increasing variety in the types of illustrations
- may be several illustrations on each page
- combinations of photography and drawing may be used
- diagrams and maps continue to be used to label and organise information

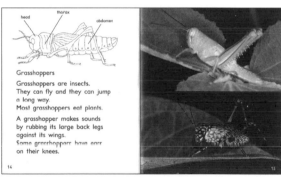

Examples of transitional texts (levels 12–17): *Animal Diggers* (pp. 4–5) and *Insects* (pp. 14–15) (Alphakids), Sundance 1999.

Extending reading behaviours and text features

Books at the extending phase of reading may have several ideas in the plot and are often episodic. If the text is episodic there is often repetition of text. Sentences are generally longer and there is variety in sentence length. There are usually between four and eight lines of text on a page, although sometimes there may be up to eleven lines of text on one page with an illustration on the opposite page. The reader has to rely on the text to find the meaning as there is less support in the illustrations. New vocabulary and new concepts are introduced at an increasing rate. A variety of text types are introduced and knowledge of the different ways of using texts becomes even more important.

Children are encouraged to integrate information from multiple sources, and fluent reading occurs. At this level, the children may choose to read silently and will revert back to reading aloud if the text becomes difficult.

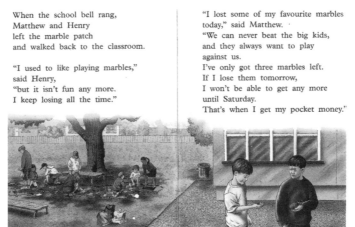

When the school bell rang,
Matthew and Henry
left the marble patch
and walked back to the classroom.

"I used to like playing marbles,"
said Henry,
"but it isn't fun any more.
I keep losing all the time."

"I lost some of my favourite marbles
today," said Matthew.
"We can never beat the big kids,
and they always want to play
against us.
I've only got three marbles left.
If I lose them tomorrow,
I won't be able to get any more
until Saturday.
That's when I get my pocket money."

An example of an extending text: *The Marble Patch* (Rigby PM Collection), Rigby 1998, pp2–3

Some cautions about text levels

Levelling books enables the teacher to build careful scaffolding of reading behaviour; however, the levels of text gradient have fine distinctions of difficulty and in the classroom it may be more pragmatic to use broader groups.

Emergent	A	levels 1–2
Gold	B	levels 3–5
Early	C	levels 6–8
Red	D	levels 9–11
Transitional	E	levels 12–14
Blue	F	levels 15–17
Extending	G	levels 18–20
Green	H	levels 21–23

An example of a broader grouping of text levels

Text levels can provide a scaffold for supporting children's reading development and they are useful guides for this purpose. However, when measuring reading progress with book levels it is important to keep in mind that the interval or gaps between levels are not equal. There is quite a jump between level 2 and 3 where children move from two lines of text to three or more. On the other hand, there is a very small degree of change between levels 11 and 12. Comparing a child's reading behaviours in levels 1 and 2 with those in levels 11 and 12 with the expectation of showing equal distance in literacy growth is unproductive.

Individual children's world view, history and experiences will make some books easier than others. A book about spiders with complex syntax may be read well by a person interested in spiders. Gender, race and other cultural experiences will also affect how easy or difficult a child perceives a book to be.

Children do not develop literacy in the same neat, linear, sequential way with each individual at the same stage. Some children will need to read many books at the emergent levels to build confidence and some will move quickly to the extending phase. Some children will choose one information source, such as visual cues, over others like meaning and sentence structure and will need careful guidance with easier texts to move along from this narrow reliance on one cue.

The level of text difficulty needs to be considered alongside the quality of the book, the story, the plot and congruence with children's worlds. It is quite difficult to write a book with twenty words that has a great plot and a high interest level – but it can be done.

	Book levels	Approximate reading age
Emergent	1–2	4.5–5.5
	3–5	5.0–5.5
Early	6–8	5.5–6.0
	9–11	5.5–6.0
Transitional	12–13	5.5–6.0
	14–15	6.0–6.5
	16–17	6.5–7.0
Extending	18–20	7.0–7.5
	21–22	7.0–8.0
	23–24	8.0–8.5
Fluent	25–26	8.0–9.0

Book levels and approximate reading age

CHAPTER FIVE

Teaching opportunities

The teaching opportunities that flow from a particular book may concern the meaning of the text, the sound and letter relationships, how the text can be read and why the author wrote the book. Reading is about code breaking and meaning making, but it is also about understanding how texts can be read and used. To be critical consumers of written texts, children need to learn to read from a critical perspective. Text critics, from the earliest time, can ask questions such as 'What does this book want me to think?', 'Why did the author write the book in this way?', 'Why were these particular characters used?', 'How else could the book end?'

Understanding the four practices of a literacy learner helps teachers to plan teaching opportunities that focus on the code or the mechanics, the meaning or what texts can mean in particular cultures, how different text types can be used and how to critically analyse texts. All readers need to understand and experience using all four practices of a reader in order to develop into fluent and flexible readers. (Four roles of a reader based on Freebody & Luke 1990: 7–16.)

meaning maker	code breaker
text user	text critic

Meaning maker

Meaning makers read to understand. They search for meaning in the illustrations, sentence structure and the print. Teachers can enhance children's comprehension of a text by asking questions that connect their prior experiences with the book.

Before children start a new book, teachers can initiate conversations which build knowledge that connects the text to children's world view and prior experiences. Connecting conversations might involve:
- building up a list of words related to the book's topic
- listing questions about the text
- building semantic webs or diagrams

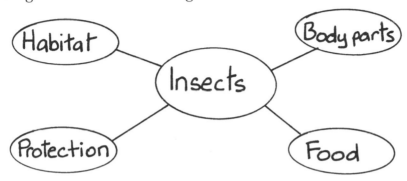

- reading a related poem or story
- sharing an experience about the topic

After reading, students could retell the story from the book. A retelling provides useful information about the child's understanding of the characters and the events in the plot. If the book is factual, then the important facts can be retold.

Comprehension questions can be posed to explore children's literal, inferential and critical thinking.

Asking questions that connect children's prior experiences with the book enhances their comprehension of a text.

Code breaker

Code breakers use what they know about sound–letter relationships, high-frequency or sight words, and oral and written language to decode print. Teachers can support the role of code breaker by providing opportunities for children to understand the alphabetic principle and develop phonemic awareness.

Phonemic awareness often occurs first of all when children become conscious of sounds in the spoken words they use. Later on, these sounds are mapped or linked to letters as children learn the alphabetic principle. Phonics is the teaching of letter–sound relationships for reading and for writing.

Activities based on letter–sound relationships support the role of code breaker.

The alphabetic principle

The alphabetic principle is the idea that written spellings systematically represent spoken words. To understand the alphabetic principle, children require some phonemic awareness or awareness of sounds. They also require letter knowledge – the name of the letter and the sounds the letter can represent.

Phonemic awareness

Phonemic awareness is the conscious knowledge of spoken words and sounds in language. The ability to hear and use the sounds in language develops from childhood right through to adulthood. For beginning readers, phonemic awareness concerns listening for words, syllables, rhyme, alliteration and phonemes. Hearing individual words is necessary for writing, and attention to the first sounds is also essential. An example of later phonemic awareness for older students or adults involves selecting the right word to create a mood or image in a song, advertisement or political speech.

Readers must have a certain level of phonemic awareness in order to take advantage of reading instruction. However, once reading instruction begins, both phonemic awareness and print knowledge increases. The more children read and write, the more their knowledge of letters and sounds develops in an interactive process. Phonemic awareness has a strong relationship to future reading development.

Playing a sound game

Letter knowledge

Knowing the letter names helps children to remember their sounds, as letter names help them to induce the sounds. For example, when using temporary spelling children use letter names to spontaneously produce words such as KAT (cat), PPL (people), JRIV (drive).

Knowledge of the alphabetic principle extends children's early reading and writing achievement. They learn to hear and write more complex consonant and vowel sounds and, as they learn to read, they map sounds to letters and letter clusters.

Analogy and 'whole-to-parts' phonics

Analogy or 'whole-to-parts' phonics involves teaching children to identify words by the word parts of onset and rime. In a syllable, the *onset* is any consonant(s) that precedes the vowel. The *rime* consists of the vowel and any consonants that come after it. Thirty-seven rimes make up many of the 500 words appearing in early reading texts (Adams 1994).

Word	Onset	Rime
I		I
itch		itch
sit	s-	-it
spit	sp-	-it
splint	spl-	-int
pie	p-	-ie
spy	sp-	-y

Readers can use onsets and rimes to identify new words – using the analogy of a known word to discover an unknown word. For example, if children meet an unfamiliar word *date*, and know the word *late*, they can use a process of analogy to work out the new word.

Teaching of whole-to-parts phonics can occur, for example, when the teacher and children have read a text and the teacher asks children to select their favourite words in the story. The teacher writes each word on a separate piece of card, or the chalkboard, highlighting letters representing an onset (eg *sm-*) or a rime (eg *-iles*). The teacher tells the children: 'These letters say /sm/' or 'These letters say /ilz/' and the words are then placed on the classroom word wall.

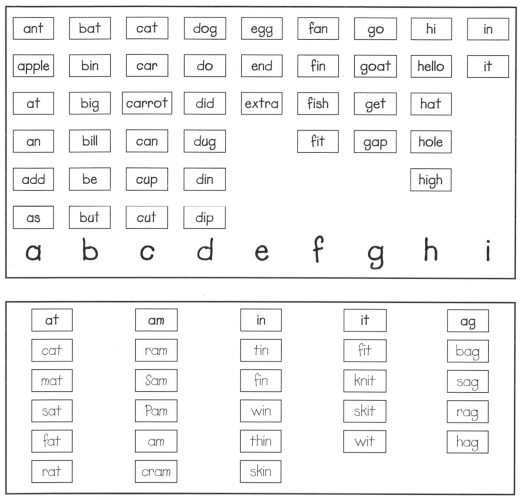

Here are two different word walls. One has words organised according to initial letters: a b c d e f g h i j. The second wall has word groups according to rime: at, am, in, it, ag, am.

As more and more words are placed on the word wall, the teacher and children can group words with similar onsets and rimes to make word families. For example, words with a 'dr' onset such as *drink, drip* and *drum* could be grouped together. The 'dr' blend can be highlighted with a pen to make recognition easier. At other times the words might be organised in word families or rimes with all the *-ink, -um* or *-ip* words grouped together.

Onset and rime is important because children make analogies with onsets and rimes in both reading and writing.

-ack	-ail	-ain	-ake	-ale	-ame	-an
-ank	-ap	-ash	-at	-ate	-aw	-ay
-eat	-ell	-est	-ice	-ick	-ide	-ight
-ill	-in	-ine	-ing	-ink	-p	-ir
-ock	-oke	-op	-ore	-or	-uck	-ug
-ump	-unk					

Common rimes

The advantages of using onset and rime in instruction for early reading are numerous:

- it is easier to distinguish initial onsets and rimes than individual phonemes
- children find rimes easier to identify than single final phonemes
- the awareness that different onsets can be spliced onto the same rime means that children can make different words
- more new words can be identified using onset and rime than the relatively low individual phoneme as the unit of analysis

Using a sentence-strip holder to match words

High-frequency words

Many words occur over and over and these words are known as sight words or high-frequency words. Reading fluency is improved if high-frequency words are recognised automatically.

Text user

Text users identify the text features and genre of a book to determine how they will read it. The purpose of a text affects the format and how the text is read. If the book is factual then reading for information is a focus. If the text is a recount the purpose is to tell what happened. The purpose of a narrative is to entertain and an information report organises and stores factual information.

Most books fit one particular text type but some books combine text types in different ways and for this reason it is important to use the features of text as general guidelines and not as rigid criteria.

There are many teaching opportunities for making explicit the knowledge children already have as text users. The description of different text features can occur during shared book reading, during modelled writing and during guided reading.

Learning to be a text user means developing a language about texts and to do this teachers can use questions like:

What kind of text is this?

Is this book a recount or a narrative?

What is the writer doing here?

Is this text an explanation of something?

If this text is a narrative, what is the problem to be solved?

Learning to be a text user means developing a language about texts

Features of common text types

The purpose and features of common text types such as recount, narrative, instruction, information report and explanation are described here so that children can explore how texts can be used.

RECOUNT

The purpose of a recount is to tell what happened and past experiences are retold.

Recount
_____

• Beginning

• Series of events

• Personal comment

• A recount usually starts with a beginning that tells the reader:
  who was involved
  where it happened
  what happened
  when it happened
  why it happened
• The series of events is usually chronological.
• There may be a personal comment to conclude.
Recounts can be personal retellings of an activity, factual retellings (eg a science experiment or a news story), or imaginative recounts (eg 'A day in space').

NARRATIVE

The purpose of a narrative is to entertain, to teach or to extend the reader's imagination. A narrative usually begins by introducing the setting, the characters and a hint of a possible problem or complication, for example 'Once upon a time there were three little pigs and a big bad wolf'.

Narrative
_____

• Beginning

• Problem

• Resolution

• The beginning of a narrative describes:
  when
  where
  who
  what may happen.
• The problem involves the main character(s) finding ways to solve the problem(s).
• In the resolution the loose ends are tied up and the characters usually get what they deserve.
Narratives can be fairy tales, fables, legends, plays, science fiction, horror stories, myths, adventure stories, realistic fiction and cartoons.

INSTRUCTION

The purpose of instructions is to tell how to do or make something.

- Instructions begin by telling the reader the goal of what to do or make.
- The materials are listed or described in order of use.
- The method for making or doing the activity is given, often in a series of steps.

Recipes, craft instructions, game rules and science experiments can be written as instructional text.

> ### Instruction
>
> - Goal
> - Materials
> - Method

INFORMATION REPORT

The purpose of an information report is to organise and store information about a class of things.

- Information reports often explore a class of living or non-living things.
- The information may be about different kinds of things.
- Information reports may examine how something is made or the aspects of something.

Information reports classify information, whereas explanation texts explain how things work.

> ### Information Report
>
> - Opening statement and classification
> - Facts such as habits, behavior, color, shape
> - Summary

EXPLANATION

Explanations explore how something works, or give reasons for why something came to be.

- An explanation begins with a statement about the object or topic.
- There are several statements of reason, explaining and elaborating on the topic.

An explanation could be a description of how a steam train works, or why Australian fauna is unique.

> ### Explanation
>
> - Statement about the topic
> - Explanation 1
> - Explanation 2
> - Explanation 3

ARGUMENT

The purpose of an argument is to take a position on some issue and justify it. The goal of an argument is to persuade someone to your point of view.

In an argument text:

```
Argument

• Statement or
  position

• Points in the
  argument with
  evidence and
  examples

• Summary
```

- sometimes background information is given before the position is stated
- the points are carefully selected and can be supported by evidence in the form of statistics and quotes. All points lead back to the statement of position.
- the points may be repeated. Sometimes there is a call for action. A resolution may be selected.

Arguments belong to a text type known as 'Exposition'. Expositions are concerned with the analysis, interpretation and evaluation of the world around us. An argument is one-sided and focuses on persuading the reader to one point of view.

Text critic

Text critics evaluate the author's purpose and the presentation of the information. Texts critics do more than read for truth and accuracy. They explore the intention of a text and how the text works on them. For example, some texts are written as advertisements to persuade people to buy toys or food. Some texts are written as cartoons to make the reader laugh and some texts are scary. Some authors write as though all children look and think the same way, and some authors can be patronising in their tone.

Text critics learn how authors make texts, and to do this they learn to read like a writer. Children learn to describe how texts are constructed to get a message across – as a leaflet, book, cartoon, poster, video or advertisement.

They may explore the intention of the author and the ways the author makes the reader feel – like a friend, like a servant or like a boss. Some books can mislead readers by leaving out information and only tell one side of the story.

Teachers support the role of text critic by providing opportunities for children to respond to what they read, to add their opinions to the information the author has offered, to challenge the premises put forth as true, and to publish book reviews and evaluations.

Questions that prompt students to read as text critics include:

What message does the author want to tell you?

What did the author have to know to write this book?

Why did the author choose to write about this topic?

What may have been left out of this book?

Does the author think you are clever or silly?

Text critics explore the intention of the author and the ways the author makes the reader feel

CHAPTER SIX

Literacy learning centres

Literacy learning centres are spaces set up in the classroom for children to practise, extend and construct new knowledge from the guided reading sessions. They are for small group work and individual learning, and they free the teacher to work in focused, uninterrupted small-group guided-reading sessions.

Literacy learning centres take advantage of the peer collaboration that children want to engage in when not directly facilitated by the teacher – children want to learn by sharing ideas and getting feedback from their peers, so why not use this productively in the classroom?

In a literacy learning centre, children engage in purposeful tasks such as guided writing, partner reading, word games and readers theatre that arise from the books read – as opposed to busy work colouring in worksheets.

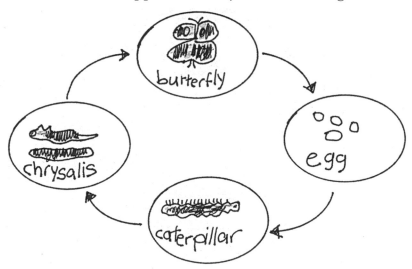

Learning centre activities involve purposeful tasks

Literacy learning centres are areas for collaborative and independent activity. Many teachers plan cooperative activities where children work with peers and there are also individual activities when necessary. For example, after a teacher had introduced a book about the life cycle of a moth to a guided reading group, the children then worked in a learning centre in pairs with one sheet of paper between two to talk about and draw the life cycle of a moth. In one pair, one child did the illustrations and the other talked about what to include, whereas in another pair the children shared the pencil and took turns:

CHILD 1: Put the moth at the top.

CHILD 2: But the moth is dead after it lays eggs and goes at the bottom.

CHILD 1: Put it at the top and go this way *(points to right)* to lay eggs and then up here it dies.

CHILD 2: What will the eggs be on?

CHILD 1: Show me the book. Look at the book.

Collaborative talk about texts is important in early literacy because the texts usually have a small number of words and a lot of information in the illustrations. Talk about the meaning of the illustrations enhances understanding and allows children to clarify their own ideas in a non-threatening way. In collaborative groups children use their own resources and draw on the resources of others. They broaden their strategies for literacy learning as they explore a variety of interactive roles such as being the director, critic, writer, illustrator and materials collector.

Class rules for collaborative work are usually constructed together with the teacher and the children. For example, for listening in the classroom the children listed the following rules:

Listening
sit still
look at the person speaking
take turns to speak
ask questions

The teacher refers to these rules often and reads them out to provide a positive model of what can be expected.

The literacy learning centre activities need to be carefully introduced so the children can work without assistance from the teacher. For example, if the card game Snap is used in a learning centre the game rules should be introduced and the game practised in small groups carefully supervised by the teacher before children play the game. Many teachers begin slowly by introducing children to the ideas and activities in one centre before moving to the next centre.

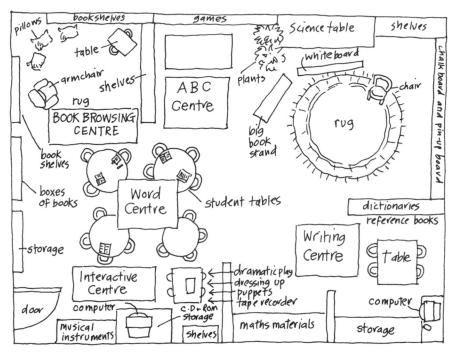

An example of one classroom layout

Group work boards

The management of learning centres is often organised with a group work board. Group work boards may begin with one or two literacy learning centres and more centres are added as children learn how to complete the activities independently.

	Monday	
Group 1		Writing ✍
Group 2	A B C **ABC**	
Group 3	Writing ✍	A B C **ABC**

Some teachers start small with an alphabet centre and a writing centre. Other teachers have many different centres: game centre, partner centre, drama centre, big book centre, author centre, computer centre, listening centre, storytelling centre, media centre, fairy tale centre and read-

LITERACY CENTRES	POSSIBLE RESOURCES

Alphabet centre
 	
ABC
	Picture cards and objects for matching
	  similar words and sounds
	Word cards
	Alphabet charts
	Plastic, cardboard, tile and/or foam
	  letters
	Alphabet books
	Individual letter books

Word centre ☺	Games, cards and CD-ROM activities High-frequency word cards Word ladders Rhyming word cards Tile letters and words Cloze with large charts Scrabble, Pictionary
Writing centre	Word processor Camera CD-ROM books and activities Pocket chart with sentence strips E-mail Book-making materials such as paper, pens, staples and cardboard

Book browsing centre	Related books, and books children can
	  read independently
	Topic books selected around other
	  curriculum areas
	Poetry, raps and rhymes

Interactive literacy centre	Pairs or multiple copies of books for
	  children to perform, or read aloud
	  together as readers theatre
	Copies of poems to read aloud
	Large print poem charts
	Poetry anthologies
	Nursery rhymes and fractured rhymes
	Listening post
	Overhead projector for visual display
	  and reading texts projected for a larger
	  audience
	Puppets
	Felt boards

around-the-room centre. In some classrooms the children choose to work at different centres and the teacher calls together small groups of children for guided reading.

In many classrooms, children are placed in several groups which rotate through activities. For example on Monday, Sam's group will do guided reading with the teacher followed by a writing activity. Adam's group will do activities in the alphabet centre, followed by guided reading. Nina's group will have book browsing then a word centre activity. Will's group has word centre and the alphabet centre, and Cass's group the interactive centre and then book browsing.

	Monday		Tuesday	
Sam's group	Guided reading	Writing centre	Word centre	Book browsing
Adam's group	A B C	Guided reading	Writing centre	Interactive centre
Nina's group	Book browsing	Word centre	Guided reading	A B C
Will's group	Word centre	A B C	Book browsing	Guided reading
Cass's group	Interactive centre	Book browsing	A B C	Word centre

Teachers can plan guided reading sessions over a one- or two-week period so that the groups meet with the teacher two to three times per week.

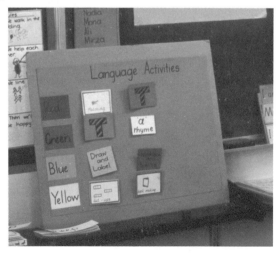

An example of a group work board

The writing centre

In the writing centre children can use frames or templates to innovate on text. They might also use pocket charts and make books using word processors, paper and pencils, crayons, and markers. The books read aloud by the teacher, big books used in shared reading and books used in guided reading may be the stimulus for guided writing. Sometimes the writing centre activities encourage creative responses. At other times there are more structured activities where children innovate on a text. All the activities can integrate writing with information technology.

Children using a computer in the writing centre

Innovating on a text

The sentence beginnings from books read in guided reading sessions can be given for emergent readers to complete, for example:

I like ...   This is a ...
I have ...   Can you see my ... ...?

Innovating on a text in the writing centre

Pocket charts

Pocket charts are strips of clear plastic in which children place cards with words and punctuation written on them. The words have been introduced during guided literacy sessions. The children arrange the words and punctuation to make sentences, and then write the sentences they have created.

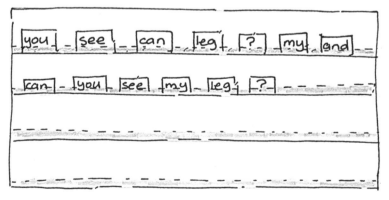

Children arrange the words and punctuation in the pocket chart to make sentences

Book making

Children can create their own books by drawing pictures and writing about the ideas. Books may be individual or created by pairs or small groups.

CAPTION BOOKS

These are books with repetitive captions where only one word changes on each page.

Examples of pages from caption books

CONCERTINA BOOKS

Concertina books are made by folding one piece of cardboard over and over until it opens like a concertina. These books are useful for drawing and writing about the main events in a book or for making drawings and writing the names of book characters.

A concertina book

CUMULATIVE BOOKS

Cumulative books start with one person contributing a line of text, then another person adding the next line, and so on.

Sam saw the cat. 🐱

Frank saw the mouse and 🐭
Sam saw the cat. 🐱

Betty saw the house, 🏠
Frank saw the mouse and 🐭
Sam saw the cat. 🐱

Vin saw the road, 〰
Betty saw the house, 🏠
Frank saw the mouse and 🐭
Sam saw the cat. 🐱

A cumulative book

PHOTO STORIES

Photo stories can be made by small groups or the whole class about local community events, school events or imaginary events. Some schools have digital cameras allowing the photographs to be loaded onto the computer with the text written alongside.

My grandma and I
walk on the beach.

A page from a photo story

TELEVISION STORIES

Children like to write about movies and cartoons they watch and this is a good place for them to do this. They can illustrate their stories or use pictures from magazines. In sharing time the children might talk about their stories and get feedback from the group.

STORY SEQUENCE

This involves picture sequences being photocopied and pasted onto pieces of card. Small groups then arrange the pictures to create a story that they can write about.

Humpty Dumpty sequence cards

STORY MAPS

Story maps show what happens in a narrative. Children may write and draw to retell the story.

Little Red Riding Hood story map

The alphabet centre

The alphabet centre is for emergent and early readers. As children move through the early and extending levels of reading, the alphabet centre will be replaced by other learning centres. The alphabet centre focuses on activities for phonemic awareness, print awareness and sound-to-letter relationship.

Using plastic letters in the alphabet centre

Phonemic awareness activities

Phonemic awareness is an awareness of the word sounds or phonemes heard in spoken language, and involves recognition of word, syllable, rhyme, alliteration and phonemes.

CLAPPING GAMES

Children can listen to songs and jingles read aloud on CDs or tape recordings and either clap to the beat or to the words in the songs.

In Clap Around the Room, a child points to an object like a pencil or a box and their partner claps the syllables *pen-cil* or *box* in the word. Consciousness of syllables is important when children begin to read and write words.

PICTURE-CARD GAMES

Picture card games in phonemic awareness focus on the sounds of the spoken word, and for this reason picture cards made from stickers, magazines and catalogues are used. The cards can be used for games of Snap, Concentration and Fish. Rhyming Snap is played with words that have a similar rime such as *cat, mat, sat;* or *sky, pie, fly.* First Sound Snap involves recognising when pictures have the same initial sound such as *fish, five, four, fan.* It is the sound of the phonemes and not the visual pattern of letters that is important here.

More complex picture-card games involve pictures or objects where one word doesn't fit, for example in rime – *fish, sand, dish* – or in first sounds such as pictures of *dog, doughnut, snake, dinner.*

Cards for a picture-card game

Print awareness activities

Print awareness involves learning about letter formation, different letter fonts, recognition and matching of letters. Letters can be cut from magazines and pasted to make collages.

Identifying letters

Sound-to-letter relationships

Sound-to-letter games can be made by writing words and illustrating them, when possible, on cards. It is helpful if a picture cue is placed near the word. Snap, Memory or Concentration, and Fish games can be played with cards. You will need 20 to 30 paired cards.

Snap games are played by pairs or small groups of children who have been dealt 5 to 10 cards. The children take turns to place a card face up on the central pile. If two cards in a row match, the first to correctly call 'Snap!' takes all the cards. The winner is the person with the most cards.

Memory or Concentration is played by pairs, small groups or individuals. A set of 20 to 30 cards with matching pairs is laid out face down. One at a time, children turn two cards over trying to make a match. If the match is correct they take the pair. If the match is incorrect they turn the cards face down again. The winner has the most pairs. The cards are then shuffled and placed face down for the next game.

Fish is similar to Snap except that 10 cards are dealt to pairs or a group of children. In turns, children try to make pairs of matching cards by asking group members for a particular card. If the person does not have the card they say 'Fish' and the person asking picks up a new card from a central pile.

Card games can be played with words with the same onset, words with the same rime or words with the same vowel sounds.

Playing card games in the alphabet centre

The word centre

The word centre is set up with a range of games and activities for children to practise making and breaking words and reading high-frequency words.

HIGH-FREQUENCY WORDS

Many teachers have the common high-frequency words – *like, was, is, the, have* – written on cardboard foot shapes attached to the floor. When the children come into the room they step on the words and say them. They play hopping games and partner games with the words. Some children have fifty or so high-frequency words under control.

A beginning list of high-frequency words is: *[child's name], I, is, like, my, am, here, a, see, and, big, can, get, me, this, the, has, to, are, go.*

The high-frequency words are written on cards which are then used to play matching games such as Fish, Concentration and Snap.

Reading high-frequency words

ONSET AND RIME

Making and breaking activities involve children making a word with plastic letters, such as *cat*, then breaking the word into its onset and rime *c-at* to make word families such as:

an	at	dog	in	but
pan	cat	log	pin	cut
can	mat	frog	fin	rut
man	sat	fog	thin	gut
	rat		grin	shut

Children can play word-sorting games, where they find words that have the same onset or the same rime, for example:

same rime – *cat, sat*

same onset – *can, candle, cake, cot*

Playing word-sorting games

Word games such as Scrabble and Bingo can also be included here. Word ladders are made when children change one letter for example:

in	go	to
pin	got	top
spin	goat	stop
	goats	step

Using the sentence maker

The book browsing centre

This is a centre for independent or collaborative reading of a range of texts previously introduced by the teacher. Books read aloud, big books from shared reading and books related to the topics discussed in guided reading also may be displayed. The book browsing centre focuses on browsing in books, following up books on topics of interest, and rereading books previously introduced in guided reading.

Sharing a book in the book browsing centre

Partner reading

In partner reading children choose a book to read together, deciding on how many pages they will read each. With some books, children might read a paragraph each, depending on the length of the book and the difficulty of the text. After reading they can take turns to retell the story to each other. They could then tell the class about the book at class sharing time.

The following is one procedure to use in partner reading.
1. Choose a book that you can read.
2. Both people look at the book.
3. Person A reads one page aloud.
4. The book is covered up and Person A retells or summarises the information on the page.
5. Person B listens and adds any information that is important.
6. Person B reads one page aloud.
7. The book is covered up and Person B retells or summarises the information on the page.
8. Person A listens and adds any information that is important.
9. This continues through the book.
10. Both person A and B then illustrate their favourite part of the book. They could invent a new story based on the book

Read-around-the-classroom

In read-around-the-classroom the children, in pairs, use a pointer and read aloud from stories that the teacher has placed along walls or hung from the ceiling.

Types of texts to include could be poetry, dictionaries, non-fiction, fables, fairy tales, alphabet books, photograph albums, books made by the class, big books, recipe books and other procedural texts, encyclopedias, manuals, magazines, comics, catalogues and plays.

The following materials encourage the reading of poems, raps and rhymes:
• charts with jingles, raps and poems for children to read
• large-print poem charts
• poems on cards
• poetry anthologies
• nursery rhymes and fractured rhymes
• Dr Seuss books

Quiet reading of a book made by children

The interactive literacy centre

In an interactive literacy centre, children interact to practise reading and writing and to respond to texts. There are multiple copies of books for pairs or small groups to read aloud. Sometimes the interactive session involves paired reading where children with similar interests and skills read together. Buddy reading occurs where older children read with younger children to share stories. Sometimes paired tutoring occurs where children are engaged in coaching each other with reading.

Reading aloud in buddy reading

There may be dramatic retellings or re-enactments of the books read; puppets and storybook characters made from felt for feltboard stories encourage dramatic responses to texts.

There maybe a tape recorder, listening post, video or CD-ROM multimedia presentation of a text and children can record music or other sound effects to use in the dramatic retelling.

Readers theatre activities can be developed where a book is read aloud by a group. The readers theatre can be performed for other children in the class. Some classrooms use video to record performances of readers theatre.

Groups of children can work together to draw story maps and create group responses in murals, models and other forms of art work.

A partner and literature circle centre could be set up for children to practise reading with buddies or partners, retell stories using various media, create new texts based on books read, develop readers theatre, and listen to texts on video, listening post or CD-ROM.

Roll movies

A roll movie is a book or story written by children and made into a series of illustrations which are rolled through a box set up like a television screen. To make a roll movie:
1. Choose a book you have read or write your own story.
2. Decide which parts of the story should go into the roll movie.
3. Get paper, pencils, paint and other colouring materials, and the roll movie box.
4. Make sure that the people in the group all have a job: illustrators, writers, storyteller, reader and roll movie turner.
5. Draw the pictures for the story onto the roll of paper (or draw on sheets of paper and tape them together).
6. Write the text under the illustrations.
7. Glue or tape the end of the roll onto the turning sticks.
8. Practise telling the story.
9. Tell the story to the class at sharing time.
10. Ask the class for feedback on the story. Which parts worked well? Which parts needed more work?

How to make a roll movie box:
1. Take a strong cardboard box
2. Cut out a screen shape in the base, leaving about 5 cm as a border on all sides.
3. Leave the sides and top and bottom intact.

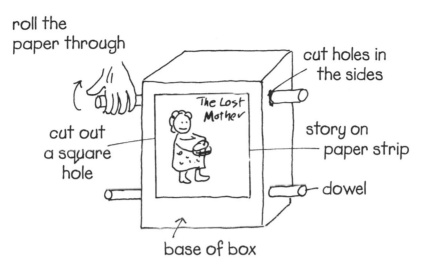

roll the
paper through

cut holes in
the sides

cut out
a square
hole

The Lost
Mother

story on
paper strip

dowel

base of box

4. Cut two holes in each side of the box leaving enough room to turn two pieces of wooden dowel. Make sure there is enough room to turn a full roll of paper.
5. Place two pieces of dowel in the holes.
6. Cover the outside of the box with adhesive vinyl.
7. Tape the beginning of the roll movie to the dowel.
8. Roll up the movie and attach the other end to the other piece of dowel.
9. Roll the paper to the beginning frame. (Based on Morrow 1997.)

Chalk talk

In a chalk talk an individual child or small group chooses a topic to make into a story. They can write their own story to be made into a chalk talk, or choose a book, a television show or movie as a starting point. In a chalk talk only one or two parts of the book are told as the child does a drawing to illustrate the ideas. If a small group is doing a chalk talk they might take turns in drawing and telling the story. It is a good idea to make sure that everyone has a job: planner, drawer, storyteller, materials maker.

It is necessary to prepare the chalk talk by deciding on which parts of the story to tell – it is important not to tell too much, just one or two events that are particularly interesting. The chalk talk can be told to another small group or the whole class. Teachers may find whiteboards are easier to work with than chalkboards.

How to prepare a chalk talk:
1. Write the story if it is your own or choose a book to use in the chalk talk.
2. Decide what parts of the story will be shown in the chalk talk.

3. Get the things you will need like chalk, paper, other drawing materials.
4. Make sure that everyone has a job like the planner, storyteller, drawer, materials gatherer.
5. Practise drawing the pictures that you will need.
6. Make any other materials that you may need.
7. Practise telling the story while the drawer does the drawing.
8. Tell the chalk talk to a small group or the whole class.
9. Talk about how well your chalk talk was done and what you may do next time. (Based on Morrow 1997.)

Readers theatre

Readers theatre is the reading aloud of texts for an audience. These can be books read in class, or stories written by children. A chorus can be added so that several readers can join in and read together.

How to prepare a readers theatre:
1. Write the story if it is your own or choose a book.
2. Decide what parts of the story will be read by which readers.
3. Get the things you will need like instruments for sound effects, music or masks.
4. Make sure that everyone has a job: narrator, props person, director, reader.
5. Practise the reading out aloud.
6. Practise the reading with sound effects.
7. Read the story to a small group or the whole class.
8. Talk about how well your readers theatre was done and what you may do next time.

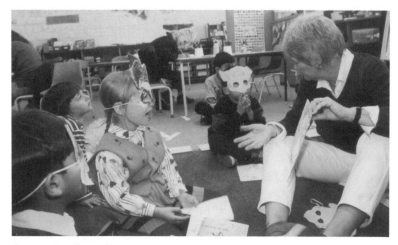

Preparing for a readers theatre

Puppets

There are many different kinds of puppets – shadow puppets, glove puppets, finger puppets, stick puppets and marionettes. Shadow puppet plays can be performed behind a screen. Puppet theatres can be made from cardboard boxes or from tables turned on their side.

Felt stories

Felt stories use characters and props made of felt that is cut out and glued together. The characters and props are placed on a felt board where they adhere. They are removed when the character is no longer playing an active role in the story. The following play can be read using simple cut-out stick puppets, face puppets (to cover children's faces) or felt puppets.

THE PANCAKE: A TRADITIONAL TALE

Characters

Pancake	Henny Penny	Goosey Poosey
Narrator	Cocky Locky	Gander Pander
Polly Wolly	Ducky Lucky	Piggy Wiggy
Manny Panny		

NARRATOR: Once upon a time Polly Wolly baked a huge, beautiful, thick pancake for her seven starving children.

POLLY WOLLY: What a wonderful pancake. I will turn you over and when you are cooked we will eat you.

NARRATOR: When the pancake heard this he was frightened. He jumped out of the pan and rolled out of the door and down the road.

MANNY PANNY: Hello Pancake. Don't roll so fast. Wait a bit. I want to eat you.

PANCAKE: Hello Manny Panny. I ran away from Polly Wolly and her seven hungry children and I must run away from you too, Manny Panny.

NARRATOR:	The pancake rolled down the road until he met a hen.
HENNY PENNY:	Hi Pancake. Why are you going so fast? Wait a bit and let me eat you.
PANCAKE:	Hello Henny Penny. I ran away from Polly Wolly and her seven squalling children and Manny Panny and I must run away from you too, Henny Penny.
NARRATOR:	The pancake rolled down the road until he met a woodcock.
COCKY LOCKY:	Hi Pancake. Why are you going so fast? Wait a while and let me take a bite of you.
PANCAKE:	Hello Cocky Locky. I ran away from Polly Wolly and her seven screaming children and Manny Panny and Henny Penny and I must run away from you too, Cocky Locky.
NARRATOR:	The pancake rolled and rolled down the road until he met a duck.
DUCKY LUCKY:	Hello Pancake. Why are you going so fast? Wait a bit and let me eat you.
PANCAKE:	Hello Ducky Lucky. I ran away from Polly Wolly and her seven starving children and Manny Panny and Henny Penny and Cocky Locky. I must run away from you too, Ducky Lucky.
NARRATOR:	The pancake rolled and rolled and rolled down the road until he met a goose.
GOOSEY POOSEY:	Slow down Pancake. Why are you in such a hurry? Wait a bit and let me eat you.
PANCAKE:	Hello Goosey Poosey. I ran away from Polly Wolly and her seven horrible children and Manny Panny and Henny Penny and Cocky Locky and Ducky Lucky. I must run away from you too, Goosey Poosey.

NARRATOR:	The pancake rolled and rolled and rolled down the road until he met a gander.
GANDER PANDER:	My dear Pancake. Why are you in such a rush? Stop! Wait! Let me eat you.
PANCAKE:	Hello Gander Pander. I ran away from Polly Wolly and her seven bawling children and Manny Panny and Henny Penny and Cocky Locky and Ducky Lucky and Goosey Poosey. I must run away from you too, Gander Pander.
NARRATOR:	The pancake rolled and rolled and rolled down the road for a long time until he met a pig.
PIGGY WIGGY:	Well hello Pancake.
PANCAKE:	Hello Piggy Wiggy. I must roll on.
PIGGY WIGGY:	Wait a while. Walk with me through this forest and we can keep each other company. It isn't very safe here.
PANCAKE:	Oh. There may be something in that. Let's go together.
NARRATOR:	They walked on until they came to a river. The pig was fat and could float across the water but the pancake couldn't get across.
PIGGY WIGGY:	Sit on my snout and I'll take you across.
NARRATOR:	And the pancake did this.
PIGGY WIGGY:	Grunt! Grunt!! Yum! Yum! What a delicious pancake.
NARRATOR:	And that was the end of the pancake.

CHAPTER SEVEN

Assessment

Assessment is done by collecting information about children's literacy development and making judgments about progress. Assessment is the basis for planning guided literacy teaching opportunities and learning centre activities.

Careful monitoring of beginning readers and writers is important because they are learning print concepts such as: written language makes sense, English written language has a pattern of left to right directionality, the written word can be matched with the spoken word, and there is a relationship between letters and sounds. Children are learning to monitor their own literacy behaviours, checking to see if what they read matches the meaning, sentence structure, word or letter.

Collecting information

During the first six weeks of school, data can be collected on a range of literacy behaviours:
- analysis of records of reading behaviours
- written language samples, drawing and writing
- concepts of book orientation, and word and letter order
- phonemic awareness
- letter identification
- retelling a narrative or recounting an experience

The most important information to collect is a record of reading behaviours which documents how a child reads a particular book. The record is an analysis of a child's reading with the child's errors or miscues which allows a teacher to examine the reading strategies and the reading behaviours used by a child at a particular point in time.

Organising information

Assessment data can be organised into baseline data and portfolios of progress.

Baseline data is a collection of information on what children can do early in the year or term. Later in the year, more information is collected and literacy progress is assessed.

Portfolios of progress are collections of work samples and records of work completed. Children place samples of their work in special folders or 'portfolios' for parents, other teachers and other children to read. The portfolio can include written work, drawings, lists of books read, records of reading behaviours (two or three examples), spelling words learnt, letters identified, and high-frequency words the child knows.

Continuous assessment enables teachers to collect writing samples, observe reading and writing behaviours, and monitor development as children are engaged in a range of activities.

Records of reading behaviours

A record of reading behaviours helps teachers find books at an appropriate learning level for children, establish a baseline for future assessment, move readers from one level to another, and report progress to parents.

The learning level of a particular text is the place where children benefit from teacher guidance. When a child reads a book at their learning level they read at between 90–95% accuracy. Marie Clay suggests that an error rate of up to one in twenty words (5%) indicates that the text is *easy* and may be read independently. A text read with an error rate of more than one in ten (10%) is a *hard* text. An error rate of between one in ten words or one in twenty words (5–10%) is at the edge of what the reader can manage with some guidance and support. This is a *learning text* (Johnson 1997). A learning text is one where the reader is challenged, and there are not enough miscues to disrupt the meaning. In a learning text, readers will also demonstrate a good understanding or comprehension of the text.

Records of reading behaviours are written on a transcript of the text. A record of reading behaviours, made on a copy of the text, provides the teacher with a clear record of the words the child can read. Teachers can place this record in an assessment portfolio for later analysis and for reporting to parents.

Taking a record of reading behaviours

A monthly record of reading behaviours is taken by:

1. selecting a book at the child's learning level that the child has not yet read
2. asking the child to read the new book aloud
3. marking carefully on a transcript of the same text the child's correct responses and miscues as she or he reads the text

The following notations can be used (based on Clay 1993; Kemp 1987; Goodman & Burke 1972).

correct	tick the word	✔ ✔ ✔ ✔ Can you see my eyes?
miscue	write the spoken word above the word in the text	✔ ✔✔ the ✔ Can you see <u>my</u> eyes?
insertion	insert the spoken word using a ^	✔ ✔ ✔✔ big ✔ Can you see my ^eyes?
omission	place a line above the word left out	✔ ✔ ✔ ✔ Can you see my eyes?
repetition	write R after the word(s) repeated	✔ ✔ ✔✔R ✔ Can you see my <u>eyes?</u>⌐
attempt	the word attempted is written above the word	✔ ✔ ✔✔ e|ey Can you see my <u>eyes?</u>
asks for help	write A above the appeal	✔ ✔ ✔ A ✔ Can you see <u>my</u> eyes?
told word	write T above the word	✔ ✔ ✔ T ✔ Can you see <u>my</u> eyes?
no response	a line is place above the word	✔ ✔ ✔ ✔ Can you see my eyes?
self-corrects	write SC after the miscue	✔ ✔ ✔ the|SC ✔ Can you see <u>my</u> eyes?

Scoring a reader's performance

Teachers can use the following scoring to evaluate a child's performance:

1. Count only the running words in a text. Running words do not include titles and subtitles.
2. Count as one error:

- miscues
- omissions
- insertions
- told words (words supplied for the reader)
- no response
- each word in a skipped line

3. Count a skipped page as one error and subtract the word count for that page from the total word count.
4. Count proper nouns read inaccurately only once. Count other words read inaccurately each time.
5. Do not count:
   - words the child self-corrects
   - words the child repeats
   - words that are pronounced differently in a child's dialect
6. Calculate the percentage accuracy for a record by subtracting the total number of miscues made from the number of running words in that text. That answer will be divided by the number of running words in the text.

   running words – total miscues = score

   score ÷ running words = percentage accuracy
7. Compare the percentage accuracy to the chart for defining instruction on each record of reading behaviours to determine whether the child is reading at the predicted instructional level.
8. Analyse the individual miscues to make a prescription for specific concepts and strategies you will explore with the child.
9. Use what you find out in steps 7 & 8 to review the guided reading groups in which children participate, to ensure that the groups with similar concepts and strategies can be grouped together for guidance.
10. Place the finished records in children's assessment portfolios to use when conferencing about the child's progress.

It is important to note that beginning readers will at times appear to slip back and regress. This is because the reader's attention may be split between different demands. Usually these slips or errors are caused by a new awareness of another concept not encountered before, which can cause reorganisation of the knowledge developed to date.

RECORD OF READING BEHAVIOURS

Benjy

✓ ✓   ✓
I like bananas

✓ ✓ or|_____
I like oranges

✓ ✓ peaches
I like pears

✓ ✓ gr_____
I like grapes

✓ ✓   ✓
I like apples

✓ ✓ ✓ ✓   ✓   ✓
I like to eat fruit salad

correct		✔ ✔ my eyes?
miscue		the ✔ my eyes?
insertion		✔ big ✔ my ^eyes?
omission		__ ✔ my eyes?
repetition		✔ R ✔ my eyes?
attempt		✔ e ey my eyes?
asks for help	A	✔ my eyes?
told word	T	✔ my eyes?
no response		__ ✔ my eyes?
self-corrects	the| SC	✔ my eyes?

Defining instruction
95–100% Move child to higher level
90–94% At learning level
0–89% Move child to a lower level

Calculating percentage accuracy

running words − total miscues = score

| 21 | − | 2 | = | 19 |

score ÷ running words = % accuracy

| 19 | ÷ | 21 | = | 90 |%

Recommendation for instruction:

The level one text is at
Benjy's learning level. He
needs to read more at this
level and use visual cues
to identify words.

Appendix

Code breaking: Sounds and letters

Emergent

- Recognise all the initial consonants and short vowel sounds (a–z)
- Recognise that vowels can make more than one sound
- Recognise capital letters
- Recognise and name each letter of the alphabet
- Identify and write initial letters in response to letter sound, word or picture
- Identify word families such as 'an', 'in'
- Be aware of alphabetic order in songs and rhymes

Early

- Practise all code-breaking work from the emergent level
- Identify, read and write short vowel sounds in letters: /a/ in *fat*, /e/ in *wet*, /u/ in *sun*, /i/ in *tin* and /o/ in *hot*
- Identify, read and write onsets and rimes
  at, an, ap, ab
  et, en, eb
  ut, un, up, ub
  in, it, ip, ib
  ot, on, op, ob
- Identify and spell words with consonant digraphs
  sh, ch, wh, th, ph
- Read and spell words with
  ck, ff, ll, ss, ng
- Blend and spell common initial consonant clusters (blends)
  bl, br, cr, dr, dw, fl, gl, gr, pl, pr, sc, scr, sk sl, sm, sn, sp, spl spr, squ st, str, shr
- Blend and spell final consonant clusters (blends)
  ld, nd, lk, nk, sk, lp, mp, sp, ct, ft, lt nt pt, st, xt, lf, nch, lth
- Discriminate, spell and read common long vowel phonemes
  ee, meet: ea seat: ey key: y pony
  oo, moon: u–e, tune: ew, threw: ue, blue
  ai, sail: ay, play: a–e name
  oa, boat: o–e, rose: ow, show
  ie, pie: i–e, kite: y, fly: igh, high

High-frequency words

First 10 high frequency words

Child's name

I   like   here   is   a   has   this   my   and

First 50 high-frequency words

a	Dad	her	make	our	this	yes
an	for	here	Mum	play	to	you
and	from	I	me	said	up	
am	get	in	my	saw	us	
at	go	is	no	see	was	
big	going	it	not	she	we	
can	have	like	of	the	went	
come	he	look	on	they	were	

Plus:
Common colour names
Numbers to ten
Days of the week

High-frequency word list for emergent and early reading

a	boy	going	into	my	ran	two
after	but	good	is	no	said	up
all	by	had	it	not	saw	us
an	came	has	just	now	see	very
and	can	have	keep	of	she	was
are	come	he	kind	old	so	we
am	could	her	know	on	some	went
as	day	here	like	one	that	were
asked	did	him	little	or	the	what
at	do	his	look	our	then	when
away	don't	house	looked	out	there	where
back	down	how	long	over	they	will
be	for	I	make	people	this	with
because	from	I'm	man	play	three	would
before	get	if	mother	put	to	you
big	go	in	me	run	too	your

Plus:
Numbers to twenty
Name and address of school
Months of the year

Read and write around the room

Read and write eight words you found when reading around the room.

Writing frame: read and write around the room   © Hill 1999

Finding facts

Write and draw four facts you learned from the book.

Writing frame: finding facts   © Hill 1999

Story sequence

Draw and write the events in the story.

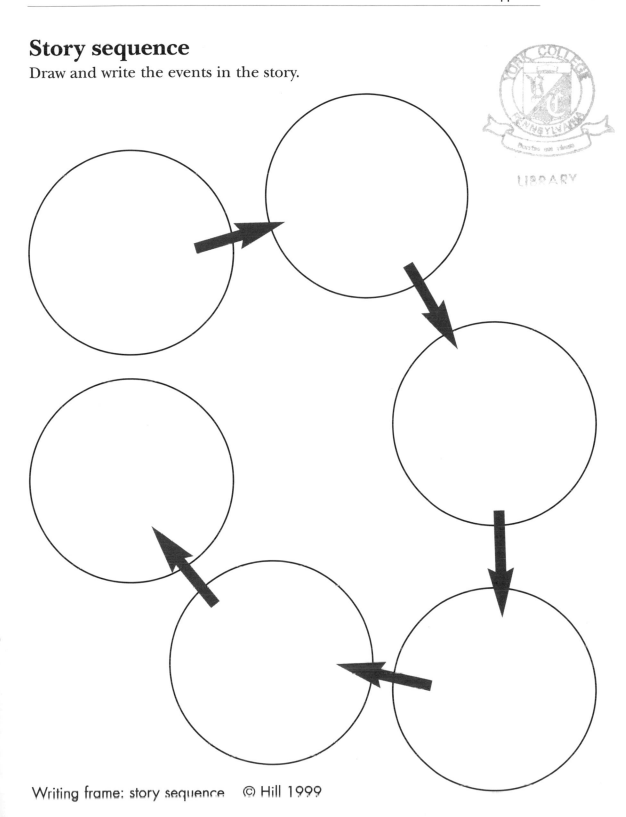

Writing frame: story sequence   © Hill 1999

Word search

Story: _____

Find all the words in the story that:

*

Draw your favourite part of the story and write about it.

* The teacher adds the features of words here.

Writing frame: word search   © Hill 1999

Recount

Beginning: who	where	what	when

Series of events

-
-
-
-
-
-
-

Personal comment

Recounts can be: *personal* retellings of an activity, *factual* retellings of a science experiment or news story, *imaginative* retellings, for example 'A day in space'.

Writing frame: recount   © Hill 1999

Narrative

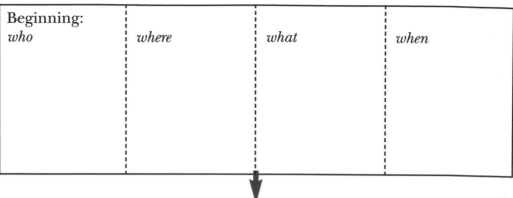

Beginning: who	where	what	when

Problem or complication: involves the main characters

Resolution: the loose ends are tied up and the characters sometimes get what they deserve

Narratives can be fairy tales, fable, legends, plays, science fiction, horror stories, myths, adventure stories, realistic fiction and cartoons.

Writing frame: narrative   © Hill 1999

Instruction

Goals

-
-
-
-

Materials

-
-
-
-

Method

-
-
-
-
-
-

Instructions tell how to do or make something

Writing frame: instruction   © Hill 1999

Report

Opening statement and classification

Facts such as habits, behaviour, colour, shape
(Diagrams and labels may be used)

-
-
-
-
-
-
-
-

Summary

Information reports classify information.

Writing frame: report   © Hill 1999

Explanation

Statement about the topic

Explanation 1

Explanation 2

Explanation 3

Explanations explain how things work.

Writing frame: explanation   © Hill 1999

Argument

Statement or position

↓

Points in the argument with evidence and examples

-
-
-
-
-
-
-

↓

Summary

An argument focuses on persuading someone to your point of view.

Writing frame: argument   © Hill 1999

References and further reading

Adams, M. 1990. *Beginning to read: Thinking and Learning about Print*. Cambridge MA: Massachusetts Institute of Technology.

Askew, B. & Fountas, I. 1998. 'Building an early reading process: Active from the start'. *The Reading Teacher*, 52 (2) pp 126–34.

Bakhtin, M. 1986. *Speech Genres and Other Late Essays*. Austin: University of Texas Press.

Clay, M.M. 1979. *Reading: The Patterning of Complex Behaviour*. Exeter NH: Heinemann.

Clay, M.M. 1991. *Becoming Literate: The Construction of Inner Control*. Portsmouth NH: Heinemann

Clay, M.M. 1993. *An Observation Survey of Early Literacy Achievement*. Auckland, Heinemann.

Clay, M & Cazden, C. 1992. 'A Vygotskian interpretation of Reading Recovery' in *Vygotsky and Education*. L. Moll (ed.). New York: Cambridge University Press.

Crawford, P. 1995. 'Early literacy: Emerging perspectives'. *Journal of Research in Childhood Education*, 10 (1) pp 71–86.

Department of Education 1985. *Reading in Junior Classes*. Department of Education, Wellington NZ.

Derewianka, B. 1990. *Exploring How Texts Work*. NSW Primary English Teaching Association.

Dorn, L., French, C. & Jones, T. 1998. *Apprenticeship in Literacy: Transitions Across Reading and Writing*. York ME: Stenhouse.

Dyson, Haas, A. 1995. 'Writing children: Reinventing the development of childhood literacy'. *Written Communication* 12 (10) pp 4–46.

Dyson, A. Haas. 1997. *Writing Superheroes: Contemporary Childhood, Popular Culture, and Classroom Literacy*. New York: Teachers College Press.

Fountas, I. & Pinnell, G.S. 1996. *Guided Reading: Good First Teaching for all Children*. Portsmouth NH: Heinemann.

Freebody, P. & Luke, A. 1990. '"Literacies" programs: debates and demands in cultural context'. *Prospect*, 5 (3) pp 7–16.

Hill, S. 1997. 'Perspectives on early literacy and home-school connections'. *Australian Journal of Language and Literacy*, 20 (4) pp 263–79.

Johnston, P. 1997 *Knowing Literacy: Constructive Literacy Assessment*. Maine: Stenhouse.

Kemp, M. 1987. *Watching Children Read and Write: Observational Records for Children with Special Needs*. Melbourne: Nelson.

Moll, L. (ed.) 1992. *Vygotsky and Education*. New York: Cambridge University Press.

Morrow, L. 1997 *The Literacy Centre: Contexts for Reading and Writing*. Maine: Stenhouse.

Moustafa, M. 1997. *Beyond Traditional Phonics: Research Discoveries and Reading Instruction*. Portsmouth NH: Heinemann.

Petersen, B. 1991. 'Selecting books for beginning readers' in *Bridges to Literacy: Learning from Reading Recovery*. D. de Ford, C. Lyons & G. S. Pinnell (eds). Portsmouth NH: Heinemann, pp. 119–47.

Piaget, J. 1955. *The Language and Thought of the Child*. New York: Meridian.

Pinnell, Su, P. & Fountas, I. 1998. *Word Matters: Teaching Phonics and Spelling in the Reading/Writing Classroom*. Portsmouth NH: Heinemann.

Richgels, D. 1995. 'Invented spelling ability and printed word learning in kindergarten'. *Reading Research Quarterly*, 30 (1) pp 96–109.

Rogoff, B. 1990. *Apprenticeship in Thinking*. New York: Oxford University Press.

Strickland, D. 1998. *Teaching Phonics today: A Primer for Educators*. Newark DL: International Reading Association.

Strickland, D., & Morrow, L. (Eds.). 1989. *Emerging literacy: Young children learn to read and write*. Newark DE: International Reading Association.

Sulzby, E. 1985. 'Children's emergent reading of favourite story books: A developmental study'. *Reading Research Quarterly*, 20 pp 548–81.

Thelen, E. & Smith L. 1998. 'Dynamic systems theories' in *Handbook of Child Psychology. Theoretical Models of Human Development*. W. Damon (ed.) R. Lerner (vol. ed.), volume 1, 5th edn. New York: John Wiley & Sons, Inc.

Tudge, J. 1992. 'Vygotsky, the zone of proximal development, and peer collaboration: Implications for classroom practice' in *Vygotsky and Education*. L. Moll (ed.). New York: Cambridge University Press, pp. 155–172.

Vygotsky, L.S. 1978. *Mind in Society: The Development of Higher Psychological Processes*. Cambridge MA: Harvard University Press.

Yopp, H. 1995. 'Read aloud books for developing phonemic awareness: An annotated bibliography'. *The Reading Teacher* 48 (1), pp 538–42.

Yopp, H. 1992. 'Developing phonemic awareness in young children'. *The Reading Teacher*, 45 (9) pp 696–703.